The Financial Crisis

and the

The Housing Bubble Nightmare

Just Facts and Figures

Who Lost and Who Gained

and

The Bailed Out Banks

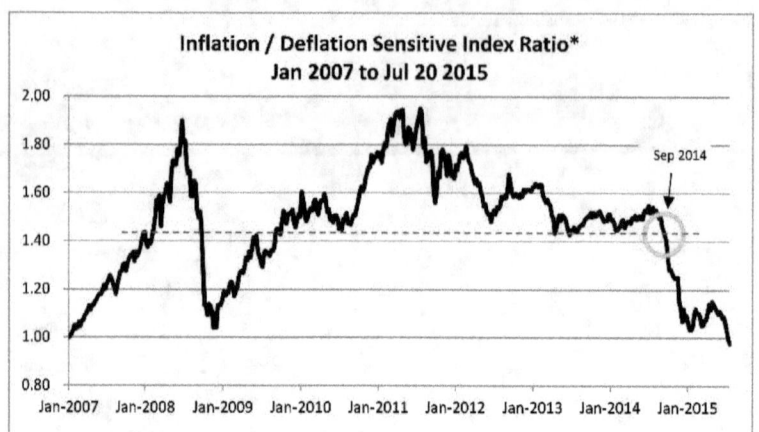

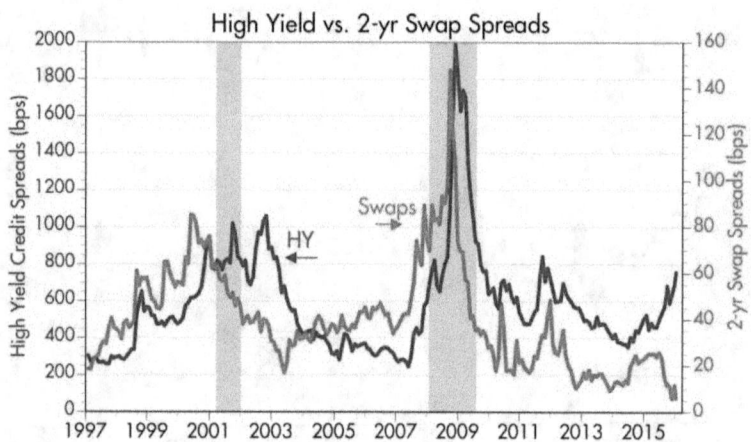

All over Europe, people that have lost all hope are actually setting themselves on fire in a desperate attempt to draw attention. Millions of formerly middle class Europeans have lost everything and are becoming increasingly desperate. Suicide and crime are skyrocketing all over southern Europe and massive street riots are erupting on a regular basis.

Unfortunately, this is just the beginning. Things are going to get even worse for Europe.

Ready for some hard facts?

Five years prior to 2008, 11 banks failed. In 2008, 25 banks failed and were taken over by the FDIC. In 2009, 140 failed.

Today the national US debt is $15.2 trillion. This amounts to $48,380 for every person living in the U.S., or $127,431 for every household in the U.S.

The velocity of money in the United States has dropped to the lowest level ever recorded. Not even during the depths of the last recession was it ever this low.

Time Magazine identified 25 people who are at most to blame for the U.S financial crisis, including Alan Greenspan, George W. Bush, Bill Clinton, the CEO of Merrill Lynch, and the American consumer.

Portugal, Ireland, Italy, Greece, and Spain have been assigned the acronym "PIIGS" and are some of the most indebted Eurozone countries. Researchers note that if a disaster happens, it will start with one of these countries.

Ireland is in massive debt because it experienced a large real estate bubble in which the government had to bail out Ireland's banks. Its debt is now 121% of its economy.

In 2004, Greece admitted that it gave misleading financial information to gain admission into the Eurozone.

Greece has a history of financial troubles -- the country's first default occurred way back in the fourth century B.C.

In the modern era, Greece has defaulted a grand total of five times -- which is only half as many times as the default leaders, Venezuela and Ecuador, have.

As of September 30, 2010, the US federal government has $56.5 trillion ($56,529,800,000,000) in debt, liabilities, and unfunded obligations.

Even though countries such as Germany and France have high output and manageable debt, the size of other countries' debt is putting the whole Eurozone in trouble. Consequently, investors don't want to buy bonds from any European country because even those who have manageable debt might have to assume responsibility for those weaker countries

The Federal Reserve System is a Privately Owned Banking Cartel. The Federal Reserve is not a government agency. The truth is that it is a privately owned central bank. It is owned by the banks that are members of the Federal Reserve system. We do not know how much of the system each bank owns, because that has never been disclosed to the American people.

In February, U.S. housing starts experienced their largest decline in 27 years

Today, the average U.S. household that has at least one credit card has approximately $15,950 in credit card debt.

The number of new building permits fell to a new all-time record low in February. In fact, new building permits were 20 per cent lower during February 2011 than they were in February 2010

According to Dr. Housing Bubble, there have been "nearly 8 million homes lost to foreclosure since the homeownership rate peaked in 2004".

As of the end of 2010, 23.1 per cent of all U.S. homeowners with a mortgage owed more on their homes than their homes were worth

According to Kathryn J. Edin and H. Luke Shaefer, the authors of a new book entitled "$2.00 a Day: Living on Almost Nothing in America", there are 1.5 million "ultrapoor" households in the United States that live on less than two dollars a day. That number has doubled since 1996.

At least 8 million Americans are at least one month behind on their mortgage payments

46 million Americans use food banks each year, and lines start forming at some U.S. food banks as early as 6:30 in the morning because people want to get something before the food supplies run out.

It is estimated that there are about 5 million homeowners in the United States that are at least two months behind on their mortgages

If you have no debt and you also have ten dollars in your pocket, that gives you a greater net worth than about 25 percent of all Americans.

18 per cent of all the homes in the state of Florida are sitting vacant. That number is 63 per cent larger than it was just 10 years ago

In 2007, about one out of every eight children in America was on food stamps. Today, that number is one out of every five.

Over the next 10 years, the U.S. government expects to pay out $45.7 trillion; however, it expects to bring in only $39 trillion. To make up this difference, the government will likely need to raise taxes on much of the population, cut its spending, and cut back on Medicare and Social Security.

In 2011, investors in global stock markets lost $6.3 trillion in wealth mainly due to fears of a Eurozone breakup.

In the state of Arizona, approximately 16 per cent of all homes are now sitting vacant

The total amount of student loan debt in the United States has risen to a whopping 1.2 trillion dollars. If you can believe it, that total has more than doubled over the past decade.

Right now, there are approximately 40 million Americans that are paying off student loan debt. For many of them, they will keep making payments on this debt until they are senior citizens.

The former Bear Stearns CEO who walked away with over $300 million plays high-stakes bridge in retirement. Jimmy Cayne oversaw Bear Stearns's massive gambling on home loans and related financial products prior to the company's collapse.

Celia Chen of Moody's Analytics projects that home prices in Florida are going to fall another 11 per cent

In total, approximately 11 per cent of all homes in the United States are currently standing empty

The real beneficiaries of the government bailout of financial institutions weren't their stockholders — it was their lenders.

The IMF claims that China will overtake the U.S. as the world's leading economic power in 2016.i

The Federal Reserve System is a Perpetual Debt Machine. As long as the Federal Reserve System exists, U.S. government debt will continue to go up and up and up. This runs contrary to the conventional wisdom that Democrats and Republicans would have us believe, but unfortunately it is true. The way our system works, whenever more money is created more debt is created as well.

In Dayton, Ohio today 18.9 per cent of all homes are now standing empty. 21.5 per cent of all homes in New Orleans, Louisiana are currently standing vacant

The Federal Reserve Can Bail Out Whoever It Wants To With No Accountability. The American people got so upset about the bailouts that Congress gave to the Wall Street banks and to the big automakers, but did you know that the biggest bailouts of all were given out by the Federal Reserve? Thanks to a very limited audit of the Federal Reserve that Congress approved a while back, we learned that the Fed made trillions of dollars in secret bailout loans to the big Wall Street banks during the last financial crisis. They even secretly loaned out hundreds of billions of dollars to foreign banks. According to the results of the limited Fed audit mentioned above, a total of $16.1 trillion in secret loans were made by the Federal Reserve between December 1, 2007 and July 21, 2010.

Home prices in the United States declined by 5.7 per cent between January 2010 and January 2011, according to CoreLogic

The youth unemployment rate in the EU is extremely high at 20%. In Spain, it is 48%. The European Commission said that not only do young people remain the hardest hit by the crisis and its aftermath, but also that "income shocks may prove permanent.

Dick Fuld walked away with half a billion dollars and three homes. Fuld's $529 million fortune is actually a lot less than he could have been worth had he been able to cash out all of his stock before the Lehman bankruptcy. He had been paid $889.5 million in salary and stock between 2000 and 2007, and at one point his stock options were worth a full $900 million.

New home sales in the United States in January were a shocking 11.2% lower than they were in December

The top 0.1 percent of all American families have about as much wealth as the bottom 90 percent of all American families combined.

Back in 1950, more than 80 percent of all men in the United States had jobs. Today, only about 65 percent of all men in the United States have jobs.

New home sales in the United States are now down 80% from the peak in July 2005

The Federal Reserve has destroyed more than 96% of the value of the U.S. Dollar. Did you know that the U.S. dollar has lost 96.2 percent of its value since 1900? Of course almost all of that decline has happened since the Federal Reserve was created in 1913. Because the money supply is designed to expand constantly, it is guaranteed that all of our dollars will constantly lose value.

An all-time record of 2.87 million U.S. households received a foreclosure filing in 2010

When Reagan took office, U.S. debt was under $1 trillion. After he left eight years later, debt was $2.6 trillion and the U.S. had moved from being the world's largest international creditor to the world's largest debtor nation.

The number of homes that were actually repossessed reached the 1 million mark for the first time ever during 2010

The number of homeless children in the U.S. has increased by 60 percentover the past six years.

72 per cent of the major metropolitan areas in the United States had more foreclosures in 2010 than they did in 2009

According to Poverty USA, 1.6 million American children slept in a homeless shelter or some other form of emergency housing last year.

In 1996, 89 per cent of Americans believed that it was better to own a home than to rent one. Today that number has fallen to 63 per cent

9.7% of Greece's young active population is unemployed.

An astounding 48.8 percent of all 25-year-old Americans still live at home with their parents.

In 2010 sales of previously existing homes in the United States were at their lowest level in 13 years

For each of the past six years, more businesses have closed in the United States than have opened. Prior to 2008, this had never happened before in all of U.S. history.

26 per cent of all the homes sold in the United States last year were foreclosures or short sales

Three bailed out CEOs whose "golden parachutes" were worth a combined $272 million are doing just fine. Charles Prince left Citigroup in 2007 following the announcement he'd lost the firm $11 billion in mortgage-backed gambles. The company paid him $28 million to leave. Stan O'Neal was fired by Merrill Lynch the same month, and the firm sent $161.5 million out the door with him. Ken Lewis left Bank of America in 2009 with a parachute payment of $83 million. All three of their firms had to be bailed out by taxpayers.

Distressed property sales accounted for nearly 60 per cent of previously owned home sales in California last

It is estimated that Bill Gates and Warren Buffet lost a collective $43 billion in 2008. However, they were not the only billionaires to have a rough year. The number of billionaires dropped from 1,125 in 2008 to 793 in 2009.

When it comes to child poverty, the United States ranks 36th out of the 41 "wealthy nations" that UNICEF looked at.

The median sale price of a home in California has declined on a year-over-year basis for five months in a row

Since the real estate peak, U.S. home values have fallen by a staggering 6.3 trillion dollars

Deutsche Bank is projecting that 48 per cent of all U.S. mortgages could have negative equity by the end of 2011

Two years ago, the average U.S. homeowner that was being foreclosed upon had not made a mortgage payment in 11 months

According to the U.S. Census Bureau, 49 percent of all Americans now live in a home that receives money from the government each month, and nearly 47 million Americans are living in poverty right now.

Right now there are now approximately 15,000 vacant buildings in the city of Chicago

According to Zillow, U.S. home prices have already fallen further during this economic downturn (26 per cent) than they did during the Great Depression (25.9 per cent)

The State of the Bailout: OUTFLOWS: $619 billion This includes money that has actually been spent, invested, or loaned. 39.6% of total: Banks and other Financial Institutions $245B: 30.3% Fannie and Freddie $187B: 12.9% Auto Companies $79.7B: 11.0% AIG $67.8B: 3.2% Other $20B

In September 2008, 33 per cent of Americans knew someone who had been foreclosed upon or who was facing the threat of foreclosure

According to Zillow, 28.4 per cent of all single-family homes with a mortgage in the United States are now underwater

According to Zillow the average price of a home in the U.S. is about 8 per cent lower than it was a year ago and that it continues to fall about 1 per cent a month

U.S. home prices have now fallen a whopping 33% from where they were at during the peak of the housing bubble

According to Zillow, more than 55 per cent of all single-family homes with a mortgage in Atlanta have negative equity and more than 68 per cent of all single-family homes with a mortgage in Phoenix have negative equity

New home sales in the United States are now down 80% from the peak in July 2005

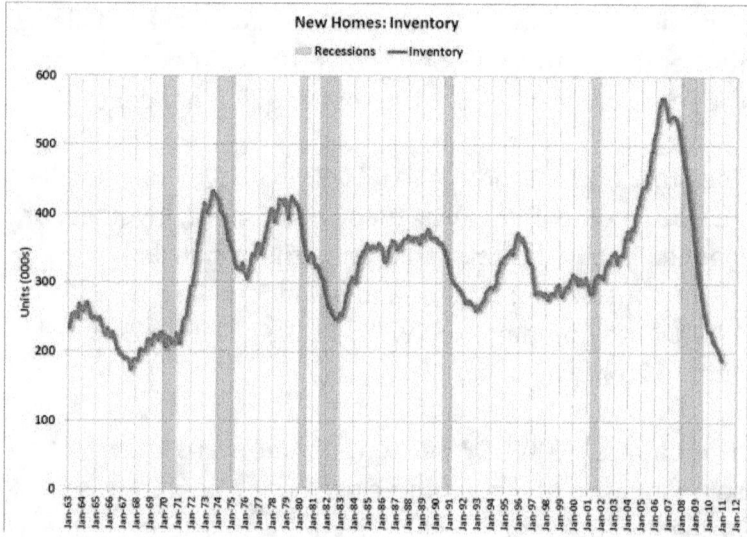

According to RealtyTrac, foreclosure filings in the United States are projected to increase by another 20 per cent in 2011

According to the Social Security Administration, 51 percent of all American workers make less than $30,000 a year.

Two years ago, the average U.S. homeowner that was being foreclosed upon had not made a mortgage payment in 11 months. Today, the average U.S. homeowner that is being foreclosed upon has not made a mortgage payment in 17 months

There is a major glut of foreclosed homes that still need to be sold off. David Crowe, the chief economist for the National Association of Home Builders, recently told CNN that the constant flow of new foreclosures being put on the market is a huge hindrance to a recovery for new home sales....

Sales of foreclosed homes now represent an all-time record 23.7% of the market

4.5 million home loans are now either in some stage of foreclosure or are at least 90 days delinquent

According to the Mortgage Bankers Association, at least 8 million Americans are currently at least one month behind on their mortgage payments

In September 2008, 33 per cent of Americans knew someone who had been foreclosed upon or who was facing the threat of foreclosure. Today that number has risen to 48 per cent

A stunningly high number of Americans are "underwater" on their mortgages right now. This could lead to an increase in the number of "strategic defaults". 31 percent of the homeowners that responded to a recent Rasmussen Reports survey indicated that they are "underwater" on their mortgages, and Deutsche Bank is projecting that 48 percent of all U.S. mortgages could have negative equity

According to a recent census report, 13% of all homes in the United States are currently sitting empty

63.5% of Greeks between ages 18 and 34 live at home with their parents.

The biggest single-day loss ever in the history of the Dow occurred on September 29, 2008, when it dropped 777.68 points, or approximately $1.2 trillion in market value.

The Federal Reserve Creates Artificial Economic Bubbles That Are Extremely Damaging. By allowing a centralized authority such as the Federal Reserve to dictate interest rates, it creates an environment where financial bubbles can be created very easily.

The United States has $2.7 trillion as its monetary base. This amount would be able to pay off only a small fraction of the over $15 trillion of U.S. debt.

Since hitting a peak of 69.2 percent in 2004, the rate of homeownership in the United States has been steadily declining every single year.

If a person spent $1 every second, that would equal to $1 million dollars in 12 days. At this rate, it would take 32 years to spend $1 billion dollars. It would take 31,000 years to spend $1 trillion dollars.

There are still 900,000 fewer middle class jobs in America than there were when the last recession began, but our population has gotten significantly larger

In 1971, the US national debt was $75 million. In 2010, the debt rate rose that much once an hour.

In 2008, U.S. households lost an estimated 18% of their net worth, equaling approximately an $11.2 trillion loss. This collapse was the largest since the Federal Reserve began tracking household wealth after WWII.

The Federal Reserve Has Become Way Too Powerful. The Federal Reserve is the most undemocratic institution in America. The Federal Reserve has become so powerful that it is now known as "the fourth branch of government", but there are less checks and balances on the Fed than there are on the other three branches.

When the U.S. debt reached 100% of its GDP in 2011, it joined Japan (229%), Greece (152%), Jamaica (137%), Lebanon (134%), Italy (120%), Ireland (114%), and Iceland (103%) as other countries whose public debt exceeds their GDP.

For the poorest 20 percent of all Americans, median household wealth declined from negative 905 dollars in 2000 to negative 6,029 dollars in 2011.

A recent nationwide survey discovered that 48 percent of all U.S. adults under the age of 30 believe that "the American Dream is dead".

On August 3, 2011, the national debt rose $238 billion, the largest one-day increase in the history of the U.S. The previous one-day record increase was on June 30, 2009, when the debt increased $186 billion.

At this point, the U.S. only ranks 19th in the world when it comes to median wealth per adult.

The U.S. government borrows approximately $5 billion every business day.

The U.S. government pays more than $1 billion each day just on interest on its debt. It spends $10 billion a day for all the services it provides.

For the first time ever, middle class Americans now make up a minority of the population. But back in 1971, 61 percent of all Americans lived in middle class households.

In 1970, the middle class took home approximately 62 percent of all income. Today, that number has plummeted to just 43 percent.

A trillion $10 bills end to end would wrap around the globe 380 times. This would still not be enough pay off the national debt.

The Federal Reserve System Is Dominated By The Big Wall Street Banks. Even since it was created, the Federal Reserve system has been dominated by the big Wall Street banks.

From August 2007 to October 2008, an estimated 20%, or $2 trillion, disappeared from Americans' retirement plans.

Greece's economic nightmare today is worse than this point in the US' Great Depression.

The 2011 debt ceiling crisis, which nearly brought the U.S. to the brink of default, has sent disapproval of Congress to the highest levels on record. An estimated 82% of

Americans disapprove of the way Congress is handling its job.

62 percent of all Americans have less than 1,000 dollars in their savings accounts, and 21 percent of all Americans do not have a savings account at all.

It has been estimated that 43 percent of all American households spend more money than they make each month.

Manufacturing activity in both France and Germany has contracted for 10 months in a row.

11.8 Percent: The unemployment rate in the eurozone has now risen to 11.8 percent – a brand new all-time high.

Manufacturing activity in Spain has contracted for 20 months in a row.

It is estimated that bad loans now make up approximately 20 percent of all domestic loans in the Greek banking system at this point.

A whopping 22 percent of the entire population of Ireland lives in jobless households.

The unemployment rate in Greece is now 26 percent. A year ago it was only 18.9 percent.

The unemployment rate in Spain has risen to an astounding 26.6 percent.

The unemployment rate for workers under the age of 25 in Cyprus. Back in 2008, this number was well below 10 percent.

Today, the poverty rate in Greece is 36 percent. Back in 2009 it was only about 20 percent.

37.1 Percent: The unemployment rate for workers under the age of 25 in Italy – a brand new all-time high.

An astounding 44 percent of the entire population of Bulgaria is facing "severe material deprivation".

56.5 Percent: The unemployment rate for workers under the age of 25 in Spain – a brand new all-time high.

57.6 Percent: The unemployment rate for workers under the age of 25 in Greece – a brand new all-time high.

Citigroup is projecting that there is a 60 percent probability that Greece will leave the eurozone within the next 12 to 18 months.

It has been reported that some homes in Spain are being sold at a 70% discount from where they were at during the peak of the housing bubble back in 2006. At this point there are approximately 2 million unsold homes in Spain.

The debt to GDP ratio in Greece is rapidly approaching 200 percent.

Top 25 People Responsible for the U.S. Debt Crisis

1. Angelo Mozilo

Cofounder of Countrywide.

2. Phil Gramm

Chairman of the Banking Committee (1995-2000); outspoken proponent of financial deregulation.

3. Alan Greenspan

Federal Reserve Chairman, disciple of Ayn Rand, admitted he made a mistake assuming financial firms could regulate themselves.

4. Chris Cox

Ex-SEC chief, blamed for lax enforcement toward investment banks like Merrill Lynch and Lehman Brothers.

5. American Consumers

Household debt in the U.S. increased to more than 130% of income in 2007, up from approximately 60% in 1982.

6. Hank Paulson

Treasury Secretary, criticized for his slow response to the financial crisis, letting Lehman Brothers fail, and for a wasteful bailout bill he pushed through Congress.

7. Joe Cassano

Founding member of AIG's financial products unit who allowed massive credit default swaps (CDS).

8. Ian MacCarthy

CEO of Beazer Homes, criticized for lying about borrowers' qualifications to get loans. Beazer Homes is being investigated by the IRS, the FBI, and the department of Housing and Urban Development.

9. Frank Raines

He was at the helm when Fannie Mae became embroiled in an accounting scandal and began making investments in subprime mortgage securities that would later go sour.

10. Kathleen Corbet

Ran the largest credit rating agency, Standard and Poor, that gave AAA ratings to risky pools of loans.

11. Dick Fuld

Criticized for leading Lehman Brothers into the business of subprime mortgages and creating toxic debt.

12. Marion and Herb Sandler

In the 1980s, the Sandler's World Savings Bank was the first to sell subprime mortgages called the option ARM. They sold Sandler's bank to Wachovia in 2006. Wachovia later collapsed when the Sandler's loan portfolio suffered huge losses.

13. Bill Clinton

Criticized by some scholars for creating a permissive lending environment.

14. George W. Bush

Criticized for embracing a philosophy of deregulation. In addition, the collapse happened under his watch.

15. Stan O'Neal

Merrill Lynch CEO. Created collateralized debt obligations (CDOs) which were made primarily from subprime mortgage bonds.

16. Wen Jiabao

Helped supply the U.S. with an unprecedented amount of debt. China is now the largest creditor to the U.S. government, to the tune of an estimated $1.7 trillion in dollar-denominated debt.

17. David Lereah

Chief economist at the National Association of Realtors who consistently claimed that the housing industry was infallible.

18. Jimmy Cayne

As CEO of Bear Stearns, Cayne took risks on questionable home loans and held nearly $40 billion in mortgage bonds that were essentially useless. Additionally, he was regularly out of town, leaving his company without effective leadership.

19. John Devany

A hedge fund manager who made it profitable for lenders to make subprime loans and sell them.

20. Bernie Madoff

His Ponzi scheme created $50 billion in losses.

21. Lew Ranieri

Former vice chairman of Salomon Brothers, considered the "godfather" of mortgage finance.

22. Burton Jablin

Helped inflate the real estate bubble by teaching TV viewers how to extract value from their homes.

23. Fred Goodwin

Considered the face of overreaching bankers everywhere.

24. Sandy Weill

Created Citigroup, which the government has already spent $45 billion trying to fix.

25. David Oddson

As Iceland's Prime Minister, he helped his country become a prime example of macroeconomic meltdown by making his country an experiment in free-market economics.

The following is a list of loan recipients....

Citigroup – $2.513 trillion

Morgan Stanley – $2.041 trillion

Merrill Lynch – $1.949 trillion

Bank of America – $1.344 trillion

Barclays PLC – $868 billion

Bear Sterns – $853 billion

Goldman Sachs – $814 billion

Royal Bank of Scotland – $541 billion

JP Morgan Chase – $391 billion

Deutsche Bank – $354 billion

UBS – $287 billion

Credit Suisse – $262 billion

Lehman Brothers – $183 billion

Bank of Scotland – $181 billion

BNP Paribas – $175 billion

Wells Fargo – $159 billion

Dexia – $159 billion

Wachovia – $142 billion

Dresdner Bank – $135 billion

Societe Generale – $124 billion

"All Other Borrowers" – $2.639 trillion

Or maybe a full list of companies bailed out during the financial crisis

Fannie Mae

Freddie Mac

AIG

Received other federal aid.

General Motors

Bank of America

Received other federal aid.

Citigroup

Received other federal aid.

JPMorgan Chase

Wells Fargo

GMAC (now Ally Financial)

Chrysler

Goldman Sachs

Morgan Stanley

PNC Financial Services

U.S. Bancorp

SunTrust

Capital One Financial Corp.

Regions Financial Corp.

Wellington Management Legacy Securities PPIF Master Fund, LP

Fifth Third Bancorp

Hartford Financial Services

American Express

AG GECC PPIF Master Fund, L.P.

AllianceBernstein Legacy Securities Master Fund, L.P.

BB&T

Bank of New York Mellon

Ocwen Loan Servicing, LLC

KeyCorp

JPMorgan Chase subsidiaries

CIT Group

Comerica Incorporated

Wells Fargo Bank, NA

State Street

RLJ Western Asset Public/Private Master Fund, L.P.

Bank of America subsidiaries (incl. Countrywide)

Invesco Legacy Securities Master Fund, L.P.

Marshall & Ilsley

Oaktree PPIP Fund, L.P.

Blackrock PPIF, L.P.

Northern Trust

Chrysler Financial Services

CalHFA Mortgage Assistance Corporation

Marathon Legacy Securities Public-Private Investment Partnership, L.P.

Zions Bancorp

Huntington Bancshares

Discover Financial Services

Synovus Financial Corp.

Lincoln National Corporation

Popular, Inc.

First Horizon National

Select Portfolio Servicing

Nationstar Mortgage LLC

Florida Housing Finance Corporation

CitiMortgage, Inc.

M&T Bank Corporation

Associated Banc-Corp

Ohio Homeowner Assistance LLC

Illinois Housing Development Authority

Michigan Homeowner Assistance Nonprofit Housing Corporation

North Carolina Housing Finance Agency

First BanCorp

City National

Webster Financial

CIT Bank, N.A.

Fulton Financial Corp

SBA Security Purchases

TCF Financial

UST/TCW Senior Mortgage Securities Fund, L.P.

South Financial Group

Wilmington Trust Corporation

GMAC Mortgage, LLC

East West Bancorp, Inc.

Sterling Financial Corp

Citizens Republic Bancorp

Susquehanna Bancshares

Valley National

Whitney Holding Corp

UCBH Holdings

First Banks, Inc.

GM Supplier Receivables, LLC

Homeward Residential, Inc.

New Jersey Housing and Mortgage Finance Agency

New York Private Bank & Trust Corp

Flagstar Bancorp

Cathay General Bancorp

Wintrust Financial Corp

PrivateBancorp

SVB Financial Group

Oregon Affordable Housing Assistance Corporation

International Bancshares Corporation

Trustmark Corp

Umpqua

Washington Federal Inc.

SC Housing Corp

Tennessee Housing Development Agency

MB Financial

Pacific Capital Bancorp

GHFA Affordable Housing, Inc.

First Midwest Bancorp

Bayview Loan Servicing LLC

First Niagara

United Community Banks

Arizona (Home) Foreclosure Prevention Funding Corporation

Ditech Financial LLC

Boston Private Financial Holdings

Provident Bankshares Corp.

National Penn Bancshares

Indiana Housing and Community Development Authority

Dickinson Financial Corp II

Western Alliance Bancorporation

Central Pacific Financial Corp

CVB Financial

Sterling Bancshares

FirstMerit Corp

Kentucky Housing Corporation

Banner Corp

Chrysler Receivables SPV LLC

Specialized Loan Servicing LLC

Signature Bank

U.S. Bank National Association

First Merchants Corp

Nevada Affordable Housing Assistance Corporation

1st Source Corp

Anchor BanCorp Wisconsin

WTB Financial Corp

S&T Bancorp

Taylor Capital

Saxon Mortgage Services, Inc.

F.N.B. Corporation

First Busey Corporation

Old National Bancorp

Park National Corporation

TALF LLC

Carrington Mortgage Services, LLC

Pinnacle Financial

Union First Market Bankshares Corporation

IBERIABANK Corp

Midwest Banc Holdings

Sun Bancorp

Plains Capital Corp

Aurora Loan Services, LLC

Westamerica Bancorporation

Integra Bank Corporation

Sandy Spring Bancorp

Mississippi Home Corporation

Heartland Financial USA

BancPlus Corporation

Hampton Roads Bankshares

First Financial Bancorp

Rhode Island Housing and Mortgage Finance Corporation

Independent Bank Corp

Columbia Banking System

TowneBank

Litton Loan Servicing LP

Bank of the Ozarks

Texas Capital Bancshares

WesBanco

Metropolitan Bank Group

Old Second Bancorp

First Place Financial Corp

Green Bankshares

Independent Bank Corporation

Virginia Commerce Bancorp

Alpine Banks of Colorado

Flushing Financial Corp

Southwest Bancorp

Superior Bancorp

MidFirst Bank

Nara Bancorp

First Bancorp

First Financial Holdings

SCBT Financial Corp

Bank United

CoBiz Financial

Wilshire Bancorp

PennyMac Loan Services, LLC

Standard Bancshares

FHA Refinance Program Fund

Lakeland Bancorp

Great Southern Bancorp

Liberty Bancshares

MainSource Financial Group

Lakeland Financial Corporation

Center Financial Corp

Community Bancshares of Mississippi, Inc./Community
Bank of Mississippi

WSFS Financial

NewBridge Bancorp

Ameris Bancorp

FNB United Corp

U.S. Century Bank

BancTrust Financial Group

Home BancShares, Inc.

Seacoast Banking Corp

State Bankshares

First South Bancorp, Inc.

First American Bank Corporation

Yadkin Valley Financial Corp

Fidelity Southern Corp

Alabama Housing Finance Authority

PNC Mortgage

The Bancorp

MetroCorp Bancshares

Cadence Financial Corp

Exchange Bank

Southern Community Financial

Sterling Bancorp

First Community Bancshares

PremierWest Bancorp

Capital Bank

Berkshire Hills Bancorp

Heritage Commerce Corp

Reliance Bancshares

Peoples Bancorp Inc.

Cascade Financial Corp

OceanFirst Financial Corp

QCR Holdings

Eagle Bancorp

Bridgeview Bancorp

Financial Institutions

First Defiance Financial Corp

TIB Financial Corp

State Bancorp

Fidelity Financial Corp

West Bancorporation

Trinity Capital Corporation

Marquette National Corp

Enterprise Financial Services Corp

Porter Bancorp

Fremont Bancorporation

Fay Servicing LLC

Encore Bancshares

The Bank of Kentucky

Southern Bancorp

First Security Group

Firstbank Corp

Centrue Financial

Pulaski Financial Corp

MutualFirst Financial

Parkvale Financial Corp

Bank of North Carolina

Royal Bancshares of Pennsylvania

Hawthorn Bancshares

Bancorp Rhode Island

Farmers Capital Bank Corp

First M&F Corp

First United Corp

Spirit BankCorp

StellarOne Corp

Tennessee Commerce Bancorp

Rushmore Loan Management Services LLC

Peapack-Gladstone Financial

Bank of Marin Bancorp

Colony Bankcorp

CenterState Banks of Florida, Inc.

Intermountain Community Bancorp

Alliance Financial Corp

Citizens & Northern Corporation

Washington Banking Company

Patriot Bancshares

HMN Financial

LNB Bancorp

Princeton National Bancorp

Peoples Bancorp of North Carolina

First California Financial Group

HF Financial Corp

Horizon Bancorp

Intervest Bancshares

Rogers Bancshares

Shore Bancshares

The First Bancorp

VIST Financial Corp

Citizens Bancshares Co.

Vantagesouth Bancshares, Inc.

Stearns Financial Services

National Bancshares

CBS Banc-Corp

Community Trust Financial Corp

Eastern Virginia Bankshares

Heritage Financial Corp

Bridge Capital Holdings

Severn Bancorp

Park Bancorporation

First Citizens Banc Corp

TriState Capital Holdings

Central Bancorp, Inc.

Premier Financial Bancorp, Inc.

University Financial Corp, Inc.

Central Community Corp

Middleburg Financial Corp

Security Federal Corp

Wainwright Bank & Trust

First Community Financial Partners, Inc.

Liberty Bancshares, Inc.

CCO Mortgage

Blue Valley Ban Corp

Residential Credit Solutions

Indiana Community Bancorp

Medallion Bank

Servis One, Inc. dba BSI Financial Services

BancIndependent

FC Holdings

AmeriServ Financial

Heritage Oaks Bancorp

Mercantile Bank Corporation

The Baraboo Bancorporation

First Guaranty Bancshares, Inc.

Unity Bancorp

United Bancorp

Citizens South Banking Corp

Florida Bank Group, Inc.

Diamond Bancorp, Inc.

First Western Financial

Commonwealth Bancshares, Inc.

Market Street Bancshares, Inc.

BNCCORP

C&F Financial Corp

Community First Bancshares

First Financial Service Corp

MidSouth Bancorp

The ANB Corporation

D.L. Evans Bancorp

Chambers Bancshares, Inc.

Community Bank Shares of Indiana, Inc.

First PacTrust Bancorp, Inc.

Carver Bancorp

Bar Harbor Bankshares

HopFed Bancorp

District of Columbia Housing Finance Agency

Sovereign Bancshares

Peoples Bancorp

First Trust Corporation

ECB Bancorp

Security Capital Corporation

First NBC Bank Holding Company

Community First Inc

Community Bankers Trust Corp

First Northern Community Bancorp

OneFinancial Corporation

Southern First Bancshares

Liberty Shares

F&M Financial Corporation (TN)

Northern States Financial Corp

The First Bancshares

Bank of Commerce Holdings

F&M Financial Corporation

First American International Corp

Guaranty Federal Bancshares

White River Bancshares Company

Timberland Bancorp

Codorus Valley Bancorp

First Federal Bancshares of Arkansas

1st Financial Services Corp

Parke Bancorp

Pacific City Financial Corp

Valley Financial Corp

CoastalSouth Bancshares, Inc.

Carolina Bank Holdings

MidWest One Financial Group

State Capital Corp.

Community West Bancshares

Stockmens Financial Corporation

Tri-County Financial Corp

BankFirst Capital Corp

First Reliance Bancshares

Grandsouth Bancorporation

Broadway Financial Corporation

Centra Financial Holdings

LSB Corp

Business Bancshares

Foresight Financial Group, Inc.

The Landrum Company

River Valley Bancorporation

Suburban Illinois Bancorp, Inc.

Nicolet Bankshares

EQUITY BANCSHARES, INC. (FIRST COMMUNITY BANCSHARES, INC. (KS))

Village Bank and Trust Financial Corp

Monarch Financial Holdings

Tidelands Bancshares

United Bank Corporation

Guaranty Capital Corporation

First National Corporation

Magna Bank

Bancorp Financial, Inc.

Sword Financial Corporation

First Texas BHC

Oak Valley Bancorp

WashingtonFirst Bankshares, Inc.

LCNB Corp

Bank of the Carolinas Corporation

Morrill Bancshares

SouthCrest Financial Group, Inc.

HCSB Financial Corporation

New Penn Financial, LLC dba Shellpoint Mortgage Servicing

Community First Bancshares, Inc.

Adbanc

Regents Bancshares, Inc.

Peoples Bancorporation

Community Financial Corp

Bankers' Bank of the West

Meridian Bank

Security State Bancshares

PeoplesSouth Bancshares

OneUnited Bank

1st Constitution Bancorp

Blue Ridge Bancshares

First Manitowoc Bancorp

FNB Bancorp

The Queensborough Company

Two Rivers Financial Group

Duke Financial Group, Inc.

Farmers Enterprises, Inc.

Alliance Financial Services

Wachusett Financial Services, Inc.

Plumas Bancorp

Citizens Bancshares

DNB Financial Corp

M&F Bancorp

TCB Holding Company

Pacific Coast Bankers' Bancshares

Cecil Bancorp

Western Illinois Bancshares

Central Virginia Bankshares

First Community Corp

Liberty Financial Services

Central Jersey Bancorp

Steele Street Bank Corporation

Allegiance Bancshares, Inc.

Mackinac Financial Corporation

Brotherhood Bancshares, Inc.

Stonebridge Financial Corp

First Capital Bancorp

First Southern Bancorp

Ridgestone Financial Services

BCSB Bancorp

Presidio Bank

Security State Bank Holding Company

First Community Bank Corp of America

Crosstown Holding Company

Northwest Bancorporation

Katahdin Bankshares

1st Enterprise Bank

Citizens Bancorp

Mission Valley Bancorp

United Bancorporation of Alabama, Inc.

Illinois State Bancorp, Inc.

North Central Bancshares

Midland States Bancorp

Heritage Bankshares, Inc.

1st United Bancorp

Blackhawk Bancorp

BOH Holdings

Center Bancorp

Central Bancorp

ColoEast Bankshares

First Bankers Trustshares

First Litchfield Financial Corp

Mid Penn Bancorp

Mid-Wisconsin Financial Services

NCAL Bancorp

New Hampshire Thrift Bancshares

Northway Financial

Stewardship Financial Corp

Uwharrie Capital Corp

Century Financial Services Corporation

HomeTown Bankshares Corporation

Greer Bancshares

Regent Bancorp

Penn Liberty Financial Corp

Coastal Banking Company

Universal Bancorp

PSB Financial Corporation

TCB Corporation

Southern Missouri Bancorp

Moneytree Corporation

Premier Bank Holding Company

Florida Business BancGroup

City National Bancshares Corporation

Cache Valley Banking Company

FCB Bancorp

Freedom First Federal Credit Union

Provident Community Bancshares

Carrollton Bancorp

First Priority Financial Corp

Elmira Savings Bank

Community Partners Bancorp

HPK Financial Corporation

Delmar Bancorp

UBT Banchares

RCB Financial Corporation

Salisbury Bancorp

Citizens First Corp

Farmers Bank

Equity Bancshares

Georgia Commerce Bancshares

United American Bank

First Freedom Bancshares, Inc.

Sonoma Valley Bancorp

BancStar, Inc.

Caliber Home Loans, Inc.

Summit State Bank

Great River Holding Company

HomEq Servicing

Private Bancorporation

Annapolis Bancorp

F&M Bancshares

IBC Bancorp, Inc.

Fairfax County Federal Credit Union

Syringa Bancorp

The Magnolia State Corporation

First Eagle Bancshares, Inc.

MS Financial

Commonwealth Business Bank

Metro City Bank

Oak Ridge Financial Services

Valley Commerce Bancorp

First Gothenburg Bancshares

Country Bank Shares

Centrix Bank & Trust

Emclaire Financial Corp

The Little Bank

BNB Financial Services Corp

Gulfstream Bancshares

GulfSouth Private Bank

Somerset Hills Bancorp

Avenue Financial Holdings

First Sound Bank

First BancTrust Corp

Western Community Bancshares

FFW Corp

Millenium Bancorp

Central Federal Corp

NC Bancorp

TriSummit Bank

Central Valley Community Bancorp

Fidelity Bancorp, Inc.

Hamilton State Bancshares

Old Line Bancshares

Chicago Shore Corporation

Heartland Bancshares, Inc.

Community Financial Shares, Inc.

Guaranty Bancorp

Idaho Bancorp

Navy Federal Credit Union

Security California Bancorp

Pierce County Bancorp

Harbor Bankshares Corporation

Monarch Community Bancorp

Premier Bancorp

Pathfinder Bancorp, Inc.

Highlands Independent Bancshares

Fidelity Federal Bancorp

Alarion Financial Services

Catskill Hudson Bancorp

Pacific International Bancorp

Liberty Bancshares, Inc. (TX)

Biscayne Bancshares, Inc.

First Intercontinental Bank

Premier Financial Corp

Citizens Commerce Bancshares

Carter Federal Credit Union

First Bank

Cardinal Bancorp II, Inc.

First Vernon Bancshares

Randolph Bank & Trust Company

Moscow Bancshares

Union Bank & Trust Company

OSB Financial Services

Centric Financial Corporation

American State Bancshares

Beach Business Bank

IBW Financial Corporation

ICB Financial

Patapsco Bancorp

Peninsula Bank Holding Co

Gateway Bancshares

McLeod Bancshares, Inc.

Howard Bancorp

Rising Sun Bancorp

IA Bancorp, Inc.

Leader Bancorp

Security Business Bancorp

Central Bancshares

FPB Bancorp

CFBanc Corporation

21st Mortgage Corporation

Seaside National Bank & Trust

United Financial Banking Companies

Waukesha Bankshares

Boscobel Bancorp, Inc

First Southwest Bancorporation

Valley Community Bank

One Georgia Bank

Legacy Bancorp

American Bancorp of Illinois, Inc.

The Private Bank of California

Highlands State Bank

Connecticut Bank and Trust Company

Selene Finance, LP

BankAsiana

Midtown Bank & Trust Company

First Choice Bank

Mission Community Bancorp

Capital Commerce Bancorp, Inc.

Franklin Bancorp, Inc.

First Resource Bank

Blue River Bancshares

Commerce National Bank

Financial Security Corp

First Express of Nebraska

Southern Illinois Bancorp

BlackRidge Financial, Inc.

Covenant Financial Corporation

AmFirst Financial Services, Inc.

Germantown Capital Corporation

First ULB Corp

York Traditions Bank

Southern Heritage Bancshares, Inc.

BNC Financial Group

First Menasha Bancshares

Alaska Pacific Bankshares

Monument Bank

Capital Bancorp

Western Reserve Bancorp, Inc

Virginia Company Bank

CalWest Bancorp

MorEquity, Inc.

Lafayette Bancorp

Hope Federal Credit Union

First Colebrook Bancorp

Puget Sound Bank

Georgia Primary Bank

Mainline Bancorp, Inc.

Community Pride Bank Corporation

CBB Bancorp

Pinnacle Bank Holding Company

Metropolitan Capital Bancorp, Inc.

BANK OF SOUTHERN CALIFORNIA, N.A. (FIRST BUSINESS BANK, N.A.)

Northeast Bancorp

Pacific Coast National Bancorp

CB Holding Corp.

Community Bank of the Bay

Pacific Commerce Bank

The Bank of Currituck

California Bank of Commerce

Capital Pacific Bancorp

Carolina Trust Bank

Hilltop Community Bancorp

Naples Bancorp

Premier Service Bank

Santa Lucia Bancorp

SBT Bancorp

Todd Bancshares

SV Financial, Inc.

Grand Capital Corporation

Investors Financial Corporation of Pettis County

Enterprise Financial Services Group

KS Bancorp, Inc.

Providence Bank

Texas National Bancorporation

Community Business Bank

Fidelity Bancorp, Inc (LA)

Peoples Bancshares of TN

Community Bancshares, Inc.

Redwood Capital Bancorp

Tifton Banking Company

Pascack Community Bank

First Financial Bancshares

Financial Services of Winger, Inc.

Pathway Bancorp

Triad Bancorp

Patterson Bancshares

AMB Financial Corp

Allied First Bancorp

CedarStone Bank

Merchants and Manufacturers Bank Corporation

AB&T Financial Corp

Mercantile Capital Corp

First Alliance Bancshares

Birmingham Bloomfield Bancshares

Bainbridge Bancshares, Inc.

Madison Financial Corp

First Bank of Charleston

California Oaks State Bank

Mountain Valley Bancshares, Inc.

Bancorp of Okolona, Inc.

Congaree Bancshares

Treaty Oak Bancorp

Border Federal Credit Union

Hometown Bancorp of Alabama

FPB Financial Corp

First Independence Corporation

Oregon Bancorp

Resurgent Capital Services L.P.

Kilmichael Bancorp, Inc.

PNC Bank, National Association

Crazy Woman Creek Bancorp

Fortune Financial Corporation

Grand Mountain Bancshares, Inc.

Lone Star Bank

Sound Banking Company

FBHC Holding Company

Citizens Community Bank

Clover Community Bankshares

Marine Bank & Trust Company

PGB Holdings

St. Johns Bancshares

Tennessee Valley Financial Holdings

Frontier Bancshares

Freeport Bancshares

Fidelity Resources Company

Bank of Commerce

Layton Park Financial Group

Redwood Financial

F & C Bancorp, Inc.

Alliance Bancshares

The Golden 1 Credit Union

Santa Clara Valley Bank

Berkshire Bancorp

US Metro Bank

Santa Cruz Community Credit Union

Omega Capital Corp

Prairie Star Bancshares

Cooperative Center Federal Credit Union

Tri-State Bank of Memphis

SouthFirst Bancshares

Worthington Financial Holdings, Inc.

M&T Bank

DeSoto County Bank

Bank of George

Regent Capital Corporation

Community First Guam Federal Credit Union

Shreveport Federal Credit Union

Deerfield Financial Corporation

Manhattan Bancshares, Inc.

Community Investors Bancorp

Scotiabank de Puerto Rico

Northern State Bank

Goldwater Bank

Community 1st Bank

Plato Holdings Inc.

Atlantic City Federal Credit Union

Pyramid Federal Credit Union

AmeriBank Holding Company

Grand Financial Corporation

Citizens Bank & Trust Company, Established 1945

CSRA Bank Corp

Green Circle Investments

Brogan Bankshares, Inc.

Ally Bank

NEMO Bancshares Inc.

IBT Bancorp

Columbine Capital Corp

CenterBank

Alternatives Federal Credit Union

Union Financial Corporation

Marix Servicing, LLC

Security Bancshares of Pulaski County

Titonka Bancshares

RoundPoint Mortgage Servicing Corporation

Ojai Community Bank

Market Bancorporation

The Victory Bank

Surrey Bancorp

TCNB Financial Corp

Nationwide Bankshares, Inc.

Atlantic Bancshares, Inc.

Northwest Commercial Bank

Fresno First Bank

Virginia Community Capital, Inc.

Hometown Bancshares

Merchants and Planters Bancshares

Wescom Central Credit Union

Monadnock Bancorp

Seacoast Commerce Bank

American Premier Bancorp

Franklin Credit Management Corporation

Southern Chautauqua Federal Credit Union

BCB Holding Company

Manhattan Bancorp

Maryland Financial Bank

Signature Bancshares

The State Bank of Bartley

Gregory Funding, LLC

Gateway Community Federal Credit Union

Gold Canyon Bank

Tongass Federal Credit Union

Hyperion Bank

Saigon National

D.C. Federal Credit Union

Regional Bankshares

Vision Bank - Texas

PFSB Bancorporation, Inc.

Sterling Savings Bank

Indiana Bank Corp

Mortgage Center LLC

Fort Lee Federal Savings Bank

Valley Financial Group, Ltd., 1st State Bank

Vigo County Federal Credit Union

ClearSpring Loan Services, Inc.

First Advantage Bancshares Inc.

Riverside Bancshares, Inc.

Southside Credit Union

Brewery Credit Union

Opportunities Credit Union

Independence Bank

Community Bancshares Of Mississippi, Inc. (Community Holding Company Of Florida, Inc.)

Calvert Financial Corp

Bank Financial Services, Inc.

BankGreenville

Butte Federal Credit Union

First Legacy Community Credit Union

Bern Bancshares

Central Florida Educators Federal Credit Union

Lower East Side People's Federal Credit Union

Urban Partnership Bank

Gregg Bancshares

Banner County Bank Corp

RG Mortgage Corporation

Seneca Mortgage Servicing LLC

UNO Federal Credit Union

First State Bank of Mobeetie

Farmers State Bancshares

Midwest Regional Bancorp

Independent Employers Group Federal Credit Union

Green City Bancshares

Quantum Servicing Corporation

Corning Savings and Loan Association

Butler Point

Colonial American Bank

Mission Federal Credit Union

Greater Nevada LLC dba Greater Nevada Mortgage

Statebridge Company, LLC

Bethex Federal Credit Union

Community Bancshares of Kansas

Kirksville Bancorp

Community Plus Federal Credit Union

Farmers & Merchants Financial Corp

Liberty County Teachers Federal Credit Union

OwnersChoice Funding, Incorporated

Technology Credit Union

Haviland Bancshares

Tulane-Loyola Federal Credit Union

SunTrust Mortgage, Inc

Banco Popular de Puerto Rico

PHH Mortgage Corporation

Northeast Community Federal Credit Union

Greater Kinston Credit Union

ShoreBank

North Side Community Federal Credit Union

United Bank Mortgage Corporation

The Freeport State Bank

Genesee Co-op Federal Credit Union

Brooklyn Cooperative Federal Credit Union

Union Settlement Federal Credit Union

Silver State Schools Credit Union

Neighborhood Trust Federal Credit Union

Prince Kuhio Federal Credit Union

FCI Lender Services, Inc.

Los Alamos National Bank

Wachovia Mortgage, FSB

Hillsdale County National Bank

AmTrust Bank, A Division of New York Community Bank

SN Servicing Corporation

Idaho Housing and Finance Association

Schools Financial Credit Union

Phenix Pride Federal Credit Union

ORNL Federal Credit Union

DuPage Credit Union

Buffalo Cooperative Federal Credit Union

IC Federal Credit Union

Citizens 1st National Bank

Western Federal Credit Union

Yadkin Valley Bank

LenderLive Network, Inc

Hill District Federal Credit Union

Episcopal Community Federal Credit Union

Great Lakes Credit Union

NJ Housing & Mortgage Finance

United Bank

Kondaur Capital Corporation

Fidelity Bank

Thurston Union of Low Income People (TULIP) Cooperative Credit Union

Heartland Bank & Trust Company

Columbia Bank

Lake City Bank

Home Servicing, LLC

Horicon Bank

Workers United Federal Credit Union

Pathfinder Bank

The Bryn Mawr Trust Company

Park View Federal Savings Bank

Aurora Financial Group, Inc

IBM Southeast Employees' Federal Credit Union

Allstate Mortgage Loans & Investments, Inc

Florida Community Bank, NA

James B.Nutter and Company

Renaissance Community Development Credit Union

Faith Based Federal Credit Union

Quicken Loans, Inc.

Iberiabank

Fresno County Federal Credit Union

Colorado Federal Savings Bank

Marsh Associates, Inc.

Axiom Bank

Ameriana Bank

Desjardins Bank

First Keystone Bank

Everbank

Fidelis Federal Credit Union

HomeStar Bank & Financial Services

Webster Bank, N.A.

Plaza Home Mortgage, Inc

Mortgage Investors Group

Purdue Federal Credit Union

Community Credit Union of Florida

Glass City Federal Credit Union

Lake National Bank

Oakland Municipal Credit Union

Union Baptist Church Federal Credit Union

Franklin Savings

California Housing Finance Agency

Cheviot Savings Bank

East End Baptist Tabernacle Federal Credit Union

Flagstar Capital Markets Corporation

First Mortgage Corporation

First Citizens Bank & Trust Company

Midwest Community Bank

Apex Bank

Bank of Camden

Land/Home Financial Services, Inc.

Georgia Housing & Finance Authority DBA State Home Mortgage

Guaranty Bank

ViewPoint Bank

BMO Harris Bank, NA

First Financial Bank N.A.

How much was the bailout in 2008?

The passage into U.S. law on October 3, 2008, of the $700 billion financial-sector rescue plan is the latest in the long history of U.S. government bailouts that go back to the Panic of 1792, when the federal government bailed out the 13 United States, which were over-burdened by their debt from the Revolutionary War.

Sources: https://projects.propublica.org/bailout/list

http://facts.randomhistory.com/debt-crisis-facts.html

http://theeconomiccollapseblog.com/archives/tag/new-home-construction

http://www.zerohedge.com/news/2013-01-09/20-facts-about-collapse-europe-everyone-should-know

Not enough Info.

How about who, when and how much

BAIL OUTS

Date	Financial Institution	City	State	Amount
10/28/2008	Wells Fargo & Co.	San Francisco	Calif.	$25,000,000,000
10/28/2008	State Street Corp.	Boston	Mass.	$2,000,000,000
10/28/2008	Bank of America Corp.1	Charlotte	N.C.	$15,000,000,000
10/28/2008	JPMorgan Chase & Co.	New York	N.Y.	$25,000,000,000
10/28/2008	Citigroup Inc.	New York	N.Y.	$25,000,000,000
10/28/2008	Morgan Stanley	New York	N.Y.	$10,000,000,000
10/28/2008	Goldman Sachs Group Inc.	New York	N.Y.	$10,000,000,000

10/28/2008   Bank of New York Mellon Corp.   New York   N.Y. $3,000,000,000

11/17/2008   Regions Financial Corp.   Birmingham   Ala. $3,500,000,000

11/17/2008   UCBH Holdings Inc.   San Francisco   Calif. $298,737,000

11/17/2008   Bank of Commerce Holdings   Redding   Calif. $17,000,000

11/17/2008   Broadway Financial Corp.   Los Angeles   Calif. $9,000,000

11/17/2008   SunTrust Banks Inc.   Atlanta   Ga. $3,500,000,000

11/17/2008   Northern Trust Corp.   Chicago   Ill. $1,576,000,000

11/17/2008   Provident Bancshares Corp.   Baltimore   Md. $151,500,000

11/17/2008   U.S. Bancorp   Minneapolis   Minn. $6,599,000,000

11/17/2008   TCF Financial Corp.   Wayzata   Minn. $361,172,000

11/17/2008   BB&T Corp.   Winston-Salem   N.C. $3,133,640,000

11/17/2008   1st FS Corp.   Hendersonville   N.C.
$16,369,000

11/17/2008   Valley National Bancorp   Wayne
N.J. $300,000,000

11/17/2008   KeyCorp   Cleveland   Ohio
$2,500,000,000

11/17/2008   Huntington Bancshares   Columbus
Ohio $1,398,071,000

11/17/2008   Umpqua Holdings Corp.   Portland
Ore. $214,181,000

11/17/2008   First Horizon National Corp.   Memphis
Tenn. $866,540,000

11/17/2008   Comerica Inc. Dallas Texas
$2,250,000,000

11/17/2008   Zions Bancorporation Salt Lake City   Utah
$1,400,000,000

11/17/2008   Capital One Financial Corp.   McLean
Va. $3,555,199,000

11/17/2008   Washington Federal Inc.   Seattle
Wash. $200,000,000

11/17/2008   Marshall & Ilsley Corp.   Milwaukee
Wis. $1,715,000,000

11/21/2008 City National Corporation Beverly Hills
Calif. $400,000,000

11/21/2008 Pacific Capital Bancorp Santa Barbara
Calif. $180,634,000

11/21/2008 Heritage Commerce Corp. San Jose
Calif. $40,000,000

11/21/2008 First PacTrust Bancorp, Inc. Chula Vista
Calif. $19,300,000

11/21/2008 Nara Bancorp, Inc. Los Angeles Calif.
$67,000,000

11/21/2008 Webster Financial Corporation
Waterbury Conn. $400,000,000

11/21/2008 Centerstate Banks of Florida Inc.
Davenport Fla. $27,875,000

11/21/2008 Ameris Bancorp Moultrie Ga.
$52,000,000

11/21/2008 Taylor Capital Group Rosemont Ill.
$104,823,000

11/21/2008 Porter Bancorp Inc. Louisville Ky.
$35,000,000

11/21/2008 Boston Private Financial Holdings, Inc.
Boston Mass. $154,000,000

11/21/2008   Severn Bancorp, Inc.   Annapolis   Md.
$23,393,000

11/21/2008   Trustmark Corporation   Jackson
Miss. $215,000,000

11/21/2008   First Niagara Financial Group Lockport
N.Y. $184,011,000

11/21/2008   Western Alliance Bancorporation   Las
Vegas   Nev. $140,000,000

11/21/2008   First Community Corporation
Lexington   S.C. $11,350,000

11/21/2008   HF Financial Corp.   Sioux Falls   S.D.
$25,000,000

11/21/2008   First Community Bankshares Inc.
Bluefield   Va. $41,500,000

11/21/2008   Banner Corporation   Walla Walla   Wash.
$124,000,000

11/21/2008   Cascade Financial Corporation   Everett
Wash. $38,970,000

11/21/2008   Columbia Banking System, Inc.
Tacoma   Wash. $76,898,000

11/21/2008   Heritage Financial Corporation
Olympia   Wash. $24,000,000

11/21/2008   Associated Banc-Corp   Green Bay
        Wis. $525,000,000

12/5/2008   Superior Bancorp Inc. Birmingham   Ala.
        $69,000,000

12/5/2008   Manhattan Bancorp   El Segundo   Calif.
        $1,700,000

12/5/2008   East West Bancorp   Pasadena   Calif.
        $306,546,000

12/5/2008   Cathay General Bancorp   Los Angeles
        Calif. $258,000,000

12/5/2008   CVB Financial Corp   Ontario   Calif.
        $130,000,000

12/5/2008   Bank of Marin Bancorp   Novato
        Calif. $28,000,000

12/5/2008   Oak Valley Bancorp   Oakdale   Calif.
        $13,500,000

12/5/2008   Coastal Banking Company, Inc.
        Fernandina Beach   Fla. $9,950,000

12/5/2008   TIB Financial Corp   Naples Fla.
        $37,000,000

12/5/2008   FPB Bancorp, Inc.   Port St. Lucie Fla.
        $5,800,000

12/5/2008   United Community Banks, Inc.
     Blairsville   Ga. $180,000,000

12/5/2008   MB Financial Inc.   Chicago   Ill.
     $196,000,000

12/5/2008   First Midwest Bancorp, Inc.   Itasca Ill.
     $193,000,000

12/5/2008   Old National Bancorp Evansville   Ind.
     $100,000,000

12/5/2008   Blue Valley Ban Corp   Overland Park Kan.
     $21,750,000

12/5/2008   Iberiabank Corporation   Lafayette
     La. $90,000,000

12/5/2008   Central Bancorp, Inc. Somerville   Mass.
     $10,000,000

12/5/2008   Eagle Bancorp, Inc.   Bethesda   Md.
     $38,235,000

12/5/2008   Sandy Spring Bancorp, Inc.   Olney Md.
     $83,094,000

12/5/2008   Old Line Bancshares, Inc.   Bowie Md.
     $7,000,000

12/5/2008   Great Southern Bancorp   Springfield
     Mo. $58,000,000

12/5/2008   Southern Missouri Bancorp, Inc.   Poplar
Bluff   Mo. $9,550,000

12/5/2008   Southern Community Financial Corp.
       Winston-Salem   N.C. $42,750,000

12/5/2008   Bank of North Carolina   Thomasville
       N.C. $31,260,000

12/5/2008   Unity Bancorp, Inc.   Clinton   N.J.
       $20,649,000

12/5/2008   State Bancorp, Inc.   Jericho   N.Y.
       $36,842,000

12/5/2008   First Defiance Financial Corp.
       Defiance   Ohio $37,000,000

12/5/2008   Central Federal Corporation   Fairlawn
       Ohio $7,225,000

12/5/2008   Southwest Bancorp, Inc.   Stillwater
       Okla. $70,000,000

12/5/2008   Popular, Inc.   San Juan   Puerto Rico
       $935,000,000

12/5/2008   South Financial Group, Inc.   Greenville
       S.C. $347,000,000

12/5/2008   First Financial Holdings Inc.   Charleston
       S.C. $65,000,000

12/5/2008　　Encore Bancshares Inc.　　　Houston
　　Texas　$34,000,000

12/5/2008　　Wesbanco Bank Inc.　Wheeling　　W.Va.
　　$75,000,000

12/5/2008　　Sterling Financial Corporation
　　Spokane　　　Wash.　$303,000,000

12/12/2008　Bank Of the Ozarks Inc.　　　Little Rock
　　Ariz.　$75,000,000

12/12/2008　SVB Financial Group　Santa Clara　　Calif.
　　$235,000,000

12/12/2008　Center Financial Corp.　　　Los Angeles
　　Calif.　$55,000,000

12/12/2008　Wilshire Bancorp Inc.　Los Angeles　Calif.
　　$62,158,000

12/12/2008　First Litchfield Financial Corp.
　　Litchfield　　Conn.　$10,000,000

12/12/2008　Wilmington Trust Corp.　　　Wilmington
　　Del.　$330,000,000

12/12/2008　The Bancorp Inc.　　　Wilmington　　Del.
　　$45,220,000

12/12/2008　Indiana Community Bancorp　Columbus
　　Ind.　$21,500,000

12/12/2008   HopFed Bancorp   Hopkinsville   Ky.
        $18,400,000

12/12/2008   LSB Corp.   Andover   Mass.
        $15,000,000

12/12/2008   Northeast Bancorp   Lewiston   Maine
        $4,227,000

12/12/2008   Citizens Republic Bancorp Inc.   Flint
        Mich. $300,000,000

12/12/2008   Independent Bank Corp.   Ionia   Mich.
        $72,000,000

12/12/2008   Capital Bank Corp.   Raliegh   N.C.
        $41,279,000

12/12/2008   NewBridge Bancorp   Greensboro   N.C.
        $52,372,000

12/12/2008   Citizens South Banking Corp. Gastonia
        N.C. $20,500,000

12/12/2008   Signature Bank   New York   N.Y.
        $120,000,000

12/12/2008   LNB Bancorp Inc.   Lorain Ohio
        $25,223,000

12/12/2008   Susquehanna Bancshares Inc.   Lititz
        Pa. $300,000,000

12/12/2008   National Penn Bancshares Inc.
      Boyertown   Pa. $150,000,000

12/12/2008   Fidelity Bancorp Inc.   Pittsburgh   Pa.
      $7,000,000

12/12/2008   Pinnacle Financial Partners Inc.
      Nashville   Tenn. $95,000,000

12/12/2008   Sterling Bancshares Inc.   Houston
      Texas $125,198,000

12/12/2008   TowneBank   Portsmouth   Va.
      $76,458,000

12/12/2008   Valley Financial Corp. Roanoke   Va.
      $16,019,000

12/12/2008   Virginia Commerce Bancorp   Arlington
      Va. $71,000,000

12/12/2008   Pacific International Bancorp Seattle
      Wash. $6,500,000

12/19/2008   BancTrust Financial Group, Inc.   Mobile
      Ala. $50,000,000

12/19/2008   Community West Bancshares   Goleta
      Calif. $15,600,000

12/19/2008   Summit State Bank   Santa Rosa   Calif.
      $8,500,000

12/19/2008   Santa Lucia Bancorp   Atascadero   Calif.
$4,000,000

12/19/2008   First California Financial Group, Inc
Westlake Village   Calif. $25,000,000

12/19/2008   Pacific City Finacial Corporation   Los
Angeles   Calif. $16,200,000

12/19/2008   Exchange Bank   Santa Rosa   Calif.
$43,000,000

12/19/2008   NCAL Bancorp   Los Angeles   Calif.
$10,000,000

12/19/2008   CoBiz Financial Inc.   Denver   Colo.
$64,450,000

12/19/2008   The Connecticut Bank and Trust Company
Hartford   Conn. $5,448,000

12/19/2008   Seacoast Banking Corporation of Florida
Stuart Fla. $50,000,000

12/19/2008   Synovus Financial Corp.   Columbus
Ga. $967,870,000

12/19/2008   Fidelity Southern Corporation   Atlanta
Ga. $48,200,000

12/19/2008   Heartland Financial USA, Inc. Dubuque
Iowa $81,698,000

12/19/2008 Intermountain Community Bancorp Sandpoint Idaho $27,000,000

12/19/2008 Wintrust Financial Corporation Lake Forest Ill. $250,000,000

12/19/2008 Marquette National Corporation Chicago Ill. $35,500,000

12/19/2008 Bridgeview Bancorp, Inc. Bridgeview Ill. $38,000,000

12/19/2008 Horizon Bancorp Michigan City Ind. $25,000,000

12/19/2008 FFW Corporation Wabash Ind. $7,289,000

12/19/2008 Fidelity Financial Corporation Wichita Kan. $36,282,000

12/19/2008 Citizens First Corporation Bowling Green Ky. $8,779,000

12/19/2008 FCB Bancorp, Inc. Louisville Ky. $9,294,000

12/19/2008 Whitney Holding Corporation New Orleans La. $300,000,000

12/19/2008 Wainwright Bank & Trust Company Boston Mass. $22,000,000

12/19/2008   Berkshire Hills Bancorp, Inc.   Pittsfield
Mass. $40,000,000

12/19/2008   OneUnited Bank   Boston   Mass.
$12,063,000

12/19/2008   Tri-County Financial Corporation
Waldorf   Md. $15,540,000

12/19/2008   Patapsco Bancorp, Inc.   Dundalk
Md. $6,000,000

12/19/2008   Enterprise Financial Services Corp.   St.
Louis   Mo. $35,000,000

12/19/2008   Hawthorn Bancshares, Inc.   Lee's Summit
Mo. $30,255,000

12/19/2008   Monadnock Bancorp, Inc.   Peterborough
N.H. $1,834,000

12/19/2008   Flushing Financial Corporation   Lake
Success   N.Y. $70,000,000

12/19/2008   The Elmira Savings Bank, FSB Elmira N.Y.
$9,090,000

12/19/2008   Alliance Financial Corporation
Syracuse   N.Y. $26,918,000

12/19/2008   Mid Penn Bancorp, Inc.   Millersburg
Pa. $10,000,000

12/19/2008   VIST Financial Corp.   Wyomissing   Pa.
        $25,000,000

12/19/2008   AmeriServ Financial, Inc   Johnstown
        Pa. $21,000,000

12/19/2008   Bancorp Rhode Island, Inc.   Providence
        R.I. $30,000,000

12/19/2008   Security Federal Corporation Aiken   S.C.
        $18,000,000

12/19/2008   Tidelands Bancshares, Inc   Mt. Pleasant
        S.C. $14,448,000

12/19/2008   Tennessee Commerce Bancorp, Inc.
        Franklin   Tenn. $30,000,000

12/19/2008   Plains Capital Corporation   Dallas   Texas
        $87,631,000

12/19/2008   Patriot Bancshares, Inc.   Houston
        Texas $26,038,000

12/19/2008   Community Bankers Trust Corporation
        Glen Allen   Va. $17,680,000

12/19/2008   Community Financial Corporation
        Staunton   Va. $12,643,000

12/19/2008   Monarch Financial Holdings, Inc.
        Chesapeake   Va. $14,700,000

12/19/2008   StellarOne Corporation   Charlottesville
        Va. $30,000,000

12/19/2008   Union Bankshares Corporation
        Bowling Green   Va. $59,000,000

12/23/2008   First Financial Bancorp   Cincinnati
        Ohio $80,000,000

12/23/2008   Bridge Capital Holdings   San Jose
        Calif. $23,864,000

12/23/2008   International Bancshares Corporation
        Laredo   Texas $216,000,000

12/23/2008   First Sound Bank   Seattle   Wash.
        $7,400,000

12/23/2008   M&T Bank Corporation   Buffalo
        N.Y. $600,000,000

12/23/2008   Emclaire Financial Corp.   Emlenton
        Pa. $7,500,000

12/23/2008   Park National Corporation   Newark
        Ohio $100,000,000

12/23/2008   Green Bankshares, Inc.   Greeneville
        Tenn. $72,278,000

12/23/2008   Cecil Bancorp, Inc.   Elkton Md.
        $11,560,000

12/23/2008   Financial Institutions, Inc.   Warsaw
        N.Y. $37,515,000

12/23/2008   Fulton Financial Corporation Lancaster
        Pa. $376,500,000

12/23/2008   United Bancorporation of Alabama, Inc.
        Atmore   Ala. $10,300,000

12/23/2008   MutualFirst Financial, Inc.   Muncie
        Ind. $32,382,000

12/23/2008   BCSB Bancorp, Inc.   Baltimore   Md.
        $10,800,000

12/23/2008   HMN Financial, Inc.   Rochester   Minn.
        $26,000,000

12/23/2008   First Community Bank Corporation of
America   Pinellas Park   Fla. $10,685,000

12/23/2008   Sterling Bancorp   New York   N.Y.
        $42,000,000

12/23/2008   Intervest Bancshares Corporation   New
York   N.Y. $25,000,000

12/23/2008   Peoples Bancorp of North Carolina, Inc.
        Newton   N.C. $25,054,000

12/23/2008   Parkvale Financial Corporation
        Monroeville   Pa. $31,762,000

12/23/2008   Timberland Bancorp, Inc.   Hoquiam
     Wash. $16,641,000

12/23/2008   1st Constitution Bancorp   Cranbury
     N.J. $12,000,000

12/23/2008   Central Jersey Bancorp   Oakhurst
     N.J. $11,300,000

12/23/2008   Western Illinois Bancshares Inc.
     Monmouth   Ill. $6,855,000

12/23/2008   Saigon National Bank Westminster   Calif.
     $1,549,000

12/23/2008   Capital Pacific Bancorp   Portland
     Ore. $4,000,000

12/23/2008   Uwharrie Capital Corp   Albemarle
     N.C. $10,000,000

12/23/2008   Mission Valley Bancorp   Sun Valley
     Calif. $5,500,000

12/23/2008   The Little Bank, Incorporated
     Kinston   N.C. $7,500,000

12/23/2008   Pacific Commerce Bank   Los Angeles
     Calif. $4,060,000

12/23/2008   Citizens Community Bank   South Hill
     Va. $3,000,000

12/23/2008   Seacoast Commerce Bank   Chula Vista
Calif. $1,800,000

12/23/2008   TCNB Financial Corp. Dayton   Ohio
$2,000,000

12/23/2008   Leader Bancorp, Inc. Arlington   Mass.
$5,830,000

12/23/2008   Nicolet Bankshares, Inc.   Green Bay
Wis. $14,964,000

12/23/2008   Magna Bank   Memphis   Tenn.
$13,795,000

12/23/2008   Western Community Bancshares, Inc.
Palm Desert   Calif. $7,290,000

12/23/2008   Community Investors Bancorp, Inc.
Bucyrus   Ohio $2,600,000

12/23/2008   Capital Bancorp, Inc. Rockville   Md.
$4,700,000

12/23/2008   Cache Valley Banking Company   Logan
Utah $4,767,000

12/23/2008   Citizens Bancorp   Nevada City   Calif.
$10,400,000

12/23/2008   Tennessee Valley Financial Holdings, Inc.
Oak Ridge   Tenn. $3,000,000

12/31/2008   SunTrust Banks, Inc.   Atlanta   Ga.
        $1,350,000,000

12/31/2008   West Bancorporation, Inc.   West Des
Moines   Iowa $36,000,000

12/31/2008   First Banks, Inc.   Clayton   Mo.
        $295,400,000

12/31/2008   CIT Group Inc. New York   N.Y.
        $2,330,000,000

12/31/2008   Fifth Third Bancorp   Cincinnati   Ohio
        $3,408,000,000

12/31/2008   The PNC Financial Services Group Inc.
        Pittsburgh   Pa. $7,579,200,000

12/31/2008   Hampton Roads Bankshares, Inc.
        Norfolk   Va. $80,347,000

1/9/2009   Commerce National Bank   Newport
Beach   Calif. $5,000,000

1/9/2009   Security California Bancorp   Riverside
        Calif. $6,815,000

1/9/2009   Security Business Bancorp   San Diego
        Calif. $5,803,000

1/9/2009   Mission Community Bancorp San Luis
Obispo   Calif. $5,116,000

1/9/2009   Valley Community Bank   Pleasanton
        Calif. $5,500,000

1/9/2009   Colony Bankcorp, Inc.   Fitzgerald
        Ga. $28,000,000

1/9/2009   The Queensborough Company
        Louisville   Ga. $12,000,000

1/9/2009   Central Pacific Financial Corp.
        Honolulu   Hawaii $135,000,000

1/9/2009   North Central Bancshares, Inc.   Fort
Dodge Iowa $10,200,000

1/9/2009   American State Bancshares, Inc.   Great
Bend   Kan. $6,000,000

1/9/2009   Farmers Capital Bank Corporation
        Frankfort   Ky. $30,000,000

1/9/2009   First Financial Service Corporation
        Elizabethtown   Ky. $20,000,000

1/9/2009   MidSouth Bancorp, Inc.   Lafayette
        La. $20,000,000

1/9/2009   Community Trust Financial Corporation
        Ruston   La. $24,000,000

1/9/2009   Independent Bank Corp.   Rockland
        Mass. $78,158,000

1/9/2009   Shore Bancshares, Inc.   Easton Md.
    $25,000,000

1/9/2009   Rising Sun Bancorp   Rising Sun   Md.
    $5,983,000

1/9/2009   The First Bancorp, Inc.   Damariscotta
    Maine $25,000,000

1/9/2009   Redwood Financial Inc.   Redwood Falls
    Minn. $2,995,000

1/9/2009   Centrue Financial Corporation   St.
Louis   Mo. $32,668,000

1/9/2009   Cadence Financial Corporation
    Starkville   Miss. $44,000,000

1/9/2009   Bank of America Corp. (Footnote 1)
    Charlotte   N.C. $10,000,000,000

1/9/2009   Crescent Financial Corporation   Cary
    N.C. $24,900,000

1/9/2009   Carolina Bank Holdings, Inc. Greensboro
    N.C. $16,000,000

1/9/2009   First Bancorp Troy   N.C. $65,000,000

1/9/2009   Sound Banking Company   Morehead
City   N.C. $3,070,000

1/9/2009   Surrey Bancorp   Mount Airy   N.C.
    $2,000,000

1/9/2009   Peapack-Gladstone Financial Corporation
Gladstone   N.J. $28,685,000

1/9/2009   Sun Bancorp, Inc.   Vineland   N.J.
$89,310,000

1/9/2009   Center Bancorp, Inc.   Union   N.J.
$10,000,000

1/9/2009   American Express Company   New York
N.Y. $3,388,890,000

1/9/2009   New York Private Bank & Trust Corporation
New York   N.Y. $267,274,000

1/9/2009   FirstMerit Corporation   Akron   Ohio
$125,000,000

1/9/2009   LCNB Corp.   Lebanon   Ohio
$13,400,000

1/9/2009   F.N.B. Corporation   Hermitage   Pa.
$100,000,000

1/9/2009   Codorus Valley Bancorp, Inc.   York   Pa.
$16,500,000

1/9/2009   Independence Bank   East Greenwich
R.I. $1,065,000

1/9/2009   GrandSouth Bancorporation   Greenville
S.C. $9,000,000

1/9/2009   Congaree Bancshares, Inc.   Cayce S.C. $3,285,000

1/9/2009   First Security Group, Inc.   Chattanooga Tenn. $33,000,000

1/9/2009   Texas National Bancorporation Jacksonville   Texas $3,981,000

1/9/2009   Eastern Virginia Bankshares, Inc. Tappahannock   Va. $24,000,000

1/9/2009   C&F Financial Corporation   West Point Va. $20,000,000

1/16/2009   Home Bancshares, Inc.   Conway Ark $50,000,000

1/16/2009   Southern Bancorp, Inc.   Arkadelphia Ark. $11,000,000

1/16/2009   Community 1st Bank Roseville   Calif. $2,550,000

1/16/2009   Pacific Coast National Bancorp   San Clemente   Calif. $4,120,000

1/16/2009   Community Bank of the Bay Oakland Calif. $1,747,000

1/16/2009   Redwood Capital Bancorp   Eureka Calif. $3,800,000

1/16/2009   Syringa Bancorp   Boise   Idaho
        $8,000,000

1/16/2009   Idaho Bancorp   Boise   Idaho
        $6,900,000

1/16/2009   Old Second Bancorp, Inc.   Aurora
        Ill. $73,000,000

1/16/2009   First Bankers Trustshares, Inc.   Quincy
        Ill. $10,000,000

1/16/2009   MainSource Financial Group, Inc.
        Greensburg   Ind. $57,000,000

1/16/2009   Morrill Bancshares, Inc.   Merriam
        Kan. $13,000,000

1/16/2009   Bar Harbor Bankshares/Bar Harbor Bank &
Trust Bar   Harbor   Maine $18,751,000

1/16/2009   United Bancorp, Inc.   Tecumseh   Mich.
        $20,600,000

1/16/2009   Pulaski Financial Corp Creve   Coeur   Mo.
        $32,538,000

1/16/2009   Dickinson Financial Corporation II   Kansas
City   Mont. $146,053,000

1/16/2009   ECB Bancorp, Inc./East Carolina Bank
        Engelhard   N.C. $17,949,000

1/16/2009 Yadkin Valley Financial Corporation Elkin N.C. $36,000,000

1/16/2009 Bank of Commerce Charlotte N.C. $3,000,000

1/16/2009 State Bankshares, Inc. Fargo N.D. $50,000,000

1/16/2009 BNCCORP, Inc. Bismarck N.D. $20,093,000

1/16/2009 New Hampshire Thrift Bancshares, Inc. Newport N.H. $10,000,000

1/16/2009 Somerset Hills Bancorp Bernardsville N.J. $7,414,000

1/16/2009 OceanFirst Financial Corp. Toms River N.J. $38,263,000

1/16/2009 Carver Bancorp, Inc New York N.Y. $18,980,000

1/16/2009 S&T Bancorp Indiana Pa. $108,676,000

1/16/2009 Citizens & Northern Corporation Wellsboro Pa. $26,440,000

1/16/2009 First BanCorp San Juan Puerto Rico $400,000,000

1/16/2009   SCBT Financial Corporation   Columbia
        S.C. $64,779,000

1/16/2009   Texas Capital Bancshares, Inc.   Dallas
        Texas $75,000,000

1/16/2009   MetroCorp Bancshares, Inc.   Houston
        Texas $45,000,000

1/16/2009   TCB Holding Company, Texas Community
Bank   The Woodlands   Texas $11,730,000

1/16/2009   Treaty Oak Bancorp, Inc.   Austin Texas
        $3,268,000

1/16/2009   United Financial Banking Companies, Inc.
        Vienna   Va. $5,658,000

1/16/2009   Centra Financial Holdings, Inc./Centra Bank,
Inc.   Morgantown   W.Va. $15,000,000

1/16/2009   Washington Banking Company / Whidbey
Island Bank   Oak Harbor   Wash. $26,380,000

1/16/2009   Puget Sound Bank   Bellevue   Wash.
        $4,500,000

1/16/2009   The Baraboo Bancorporation Baraboo
        Wis. $20,749,000

1/16/2009   First Manitowoc Bancorp, Inc.
        Manitowoc   Wis. $12,000,000

1/22/2009 Liberty Bancshares, Inc. Jonesboro
Ark. $57,500,000

1/22/2009 Commonwealth Business Bank Los
Angeles Calif. $7,701,000

1/22/2009 CalWest Bancorp Rancho Santa
Margarita Calif. $4,656,000

1/22/2009 Fresno First Bank Fresno Calif.
$1,968,000

1/22/2009 First ULB Corp. Oakland Calif.
$4,900,000

1/22/2009 California Oaks State Bank Thousand
Oaks Calif. $3,300,000

1/22/2009 WSFS Financial Corporation Wilmington
Del. $52,625,000

1/22/2009 Seaside National Bank & Trust
Orlando Fla. $5,677,000

1/22/2009 Alarion Financial Services, Inc. Ocala
Fla. $6,514,000

1/22/2009 Princeton National Bancorp, Inc.
Princeton Ill. $25,083,000

1/22/2009 Midland States Bancorp, Inc. Effingham
Ill. $10,189,000

1/22/2009   Southern Illinois Bancorp, Inc.   Carmi
    Ill. $5,000,000

1/22/2009   1st Source Corporation   South Bend
    Ind. $111,000,000

1/22/2009   FPB Financial Corp.   Hammond   La.
    $3,240,000

1/22/2009   Crosstown Holding Company Blaine   Minn.
    $10,650,000

1/22/2009   BankFirst Capital Corporation   Macon
    Miss. $15,500,000

1/22/2009   Calvert Financial Corporation
    Ashland   Mo. $1,037,000

1/22/2009   AB&T Financial Corporation   Gastonia
    N.C. $3,500,000

1/22/2009   First Citizens Banc Corp   Sandusky
    Ohio $23,184,000

1/22/2009   Stonebridge Financial Corp.   West Chester
    Pa. $10,973,000

1/22/2009   Moscow Bancshares, Inc.   Moscow
    Tenn. $6,216,000

1/22/2009   Farmers Bank   Windsor   Va.
    $8,752,000

1/22/2009   Pierce County Bancorp   Tacoma
     Wash. $6,800,000

1/30/2009   Goldwater Bank, N.A. Scottsdale   Ariz.
     $2,568,000

1/30/2009   Rogers Bancshares, Inc.   Little Rock
     Ark. $25,000,000

1/30/2009   Peninsula Bank Holding Co.   Palo Alto
     Calif. $6,000,000

1/30/2009   Central Valley Community Bancorp   Fresno
     Calif. $7,000,000

1/30/2009   Plumas Bancorp   Quincy   Calif.
     $11,949,000

1/30/2009   Valley Commerce Bancorp   Visalia Calif.
     $7,700,000

1/30/2009   Ojai Community Bank   Ojai   Calif.
     $2,080,000

1/30/2009   Beach Business Bank   Manhattan Beach
     Calif. $6,000,000

1/30/2009   Bankers' Bank of tde West Bancorp, Inc.
     Denver   Colo. $12,639,000

1/30/2009   First Soutdern Bancorp, Inc.   Boca Raton
     Fla. $10,900,000

1/30/2009   Metro City Bank   Doraville   Ga.
$7,700,000

1/30/2009   PrivateBancorp, Inc.   Chicago   Ill.
$243,815,000

1/30/2009   AMB Financial Corp.   Munster   Ind.
$3,674,000

1/30/2009   UBT Bancshares, Inc.   Marysville   Kan.
$8,950,000

1/30/2009   Equity Bancshares, Inc.   Wichita
Kan. $8,750,000

1/30/2009   Katahdin Bankshares Corp.   Houlton
Maine $10,449,000

1/30/2009   First United Corporation   Oakland
Md. $30,000,000

1/30/2009   Annapolis Bancorp, Inc.   Annapolis
Md. $8,152,000

1/30/2009   Monument Bank   Betdesda   Md.
$4,734,000

1/30/2009   Flagstar Bancorp, Inc. Troy   Mich.
$266,657,000

1/30/2009   Firstbank Corporation   Alma   Mich.
$33,000,000

1/30/2009   Guaranty Federal Bancshares, Inc.
    Springfield   Mo. $17,000,000

1/30/2009   Oak Ridge Financial Services, Inc.   Oak
Ridge   N.C. $7,700,000

1/30/2009   Nortdway Financial, Inc.   Berlin   N.H.
    $10,000,000

1/30/2009   Parke Bancorp, Inc.   Sewell   N.J.
    $16,288,000

1/30/2009   Stewardship Financial Corporation
    Midland Park   N.J. $10,000,000

1/30/2009   Community Partners Bancorp
    Middletown   N.J. $9,000,000

1/30/2009   Hilltop Community Bancorp, Inc.
    Summit   N.J. $4,000,000

1/30/2009   Adbanc, Inc   Ogallala   Neb.
    $12,720,000

1/30/2009   Country Bank Shares, Inc.   Milford
    Neb. $7,525,000

1/30/2009   Peoples Bancorp Inc.   Marietta   Ohio
    $39,000,000

1/30/2009   DNB Financial Corporation   Downingtown
    Pa. $11,750,000

1/30/2009   First Resource Bank   Exton Pa.
$2,600,000

1/30/2009   Greer Bancshares Incorporated   Greer
S.C. $9,993,000

1/30/2009   F & M Bancshares, Inc.   Trezevant
Tenn. $4,609,000

1/30/2009   Central Bancshares, Inc.   Houston
Texas $5,800,000

1/30/2009   Central Virginia Bankshares, Inc.
Powhatan   Va. $11,385,000

1/30/2009   Middleburg Financial Corporation
Middleburg   Va. $22,000,000

1/30/2009   WashingtonFirst Bank   Reston
Va. $6,633,000

1/30/2009   W.T.B. Financial Corporation Spokane
Wash. $110,000,000

1/30/2009   Anchor BanCorp Wisconsin Inc.
Madison   Wis. $110,000,000

1/30/2009   Legacy Bancorp, Inc. Milwaukee   Wis.
$5,498,000

2/6/2009   Alaska Pacific Bancshares, Inc.   Juneau
Alaska $4,781,000

2/6/2009   US Metro Bank   Garden Grove Calif.
     $2,861,000

2/6/2009   First Western Financial, Inc.   Denver
     Colo. $8,559,000

2/6/2009   Community Holding Company of Florida,
Inc.   Miramar Beach   Fla. $1,050,000

2/6/2009   Georgia Commerce Bancshares, Inc. Atlanta
     Ga. $8,700,000

2/6/2009   PGB Holdings, Inc.   Chicago   Ill.
     $3,000,000

2/6/2009   MidWestOne Financial Group, Inc.   Iowa
City   Iowa $16,000,000

2/6/2009   The Freeport State Bank   Harper
     Kan. $301,000

2/6/2009   Citizens Commerce Bancshares, Inc.
     Versailles   Ky. $6,300,000

2/6/2009   Todd Bancshares, Inc.   Hopkinsville
     Ky. $4,000,000

2/6/2009   Liberty Financial Services, Inc.   New
Orleans   La. $5,645,000

2/6/2009   Mercantile Capital Corp.   Boston
     Mass. $3,500,000

2/6/2009   Monarch Community Bancorp, Inc.
Coldwater   Mich. $6,785,000

2/6/2009   The First Bancshares, Inc.   Hattiesburg
Miss. $5,000,000

2/6/2009   Carolina Trust Bank   Lincolnton   N.C.
$4,000,000

2/6/2009   F & M Financial Corporation Salisbury
N.C. $17,000,000

2/6/2009   The Bank of Currituck Moyock   N.C.
$4,021,000

2/6/2009   Centrix Bank & Trust Bedford   N.H.
$7,500,000

2/6/2009   Lakeland Bancorp, Inc.   Oak Ridge
N.J. $59,000,000

2/6/2009   Pascack Community Bank   Westwood
N.J. $3,756,000

2/6/2009   First Express of Nebraska, Inc.   Gering
Neb. $5,000,000

2/6/2009   Banner County Ban Corporation
Harrisburg   Neb. $795,000

2/6/2009   Hyperion Bank   Philadelphia Pa.
$1,552,000

2/6/2009   Stockmens Financial Corporation   Rapid City   S.D. $15,568,000

2/6/2009   CedarStone Bank   Lebanon   Tenn. $3,564,000

2/6/2009   Lone Star Bank   Houston   Texas $3,072,000

2/6/2009   First Market Bank, FSB   Richmond   Va. $33,900,000

2/6/2009   First Bank of Charleston, Inc. Charleston   W.Va. $3,345,000

2/13/2009   Corning Savings and Loan Association   Corning   Ark. $638,000

2/13/2009   Westamerica Bancorporation   San Rafael Calif. $83,726,000

2/13/2009   1st Enterprise Bank   Los Angeles   Calif. $4,400,000

2/13/2009   Santa Clara Valley Bank, N.A. Santa Paula   Calif. $2,900,000

2/13/2009   First Choice Bank   Cerritos   Calif. $2,200,000

2/13/2009   ColoEast Bankshares, Inc.   Lamar Colo. $10,000,000

2/13/2009   QCR Holdings, Inc.   Moline   Ill.
$38,237,000

2/13/2009   Bern Bancshares, Inc. Bern   Kan.
$985,000

2/13/2009   The Bank of Kentucky Financial Corporation
Crestview Hills   Ky. $34,000,000

2/13/2009   Hometown Bancshares, Inc.   Corbin Ky.
$1,900,000

2/13/2009   Carrollton Bancorp   Baltimore   Md.
$9,201,000

2/13/2009   State Capital Corporation   Greenwood
Miss. $15,000,000

2/13/2009   DeSoto County Bank   Horn Lake   Miss.
$1,173,000

2/13/2009   Security Bancshares of Pulaski County, Inc.
Waynesville   Mo. $2,152,000

2/13/2009   Reliance Bancshares, Inc.   Frontenac
Mo. $40,000,000

2/13/2009   Gregg Bancshares, Inc.   Ozark   Mo.
$825,000

2/13/2009   Midwest Regional Bancorp, Inc.   Festus
Mo. $700,000

2/13/2009   Liberty Bancshares, Inc.   Springfield Mo. $21,900,000

2/13/2009   FNB United Corp.   Asheboro   N.C. $51,500,000

2/13/2009   PremierWest Bancorp   Medford Ore. $41,400,000

2/13/2009   Meridian Bank   Devon Pa. $6,200,000

2/13/2009   BankGreenville   Greenville   S.C. $1,000,000

2/13/2009   Regional Bankshares, Inc.   Hartsville S.C. $1,500,000

2/13/2009   F&M Financial Corp. Clarksville   Tenn. $17,243,000

2/13/2009   Peoples Bancorp   Lynden   Wash. $18,000,000

2/13/2009   Northwest Bancorporation, Inc. Spokane   Wash. $10,500,000

2/13/2009   Northwest Commercial Bank Lakewood Wash. $1,992,000

2/13/2009   First Menasha Bancshares, Inc. Neenah   Wis. $4,797,000

2/13/2009   Financial Security Corporation   Basin
        Wyo. $5,000,000

2/20/2009   Hometown Bancorp of Alabama, Inc.
        Oneonta   Ala. $3,250,000

2/20/2009   White River Bancshares Company
        Fayetteville   Ark. $16,800,000

2/20/2009   Sonoma Valley Bancorp   Sonoma
        Calif. $8,653,000

2/20/2009   The Private Bank of California   Los
Angeles   Calif. $5,450,000

2/20/2009   United American Bank   San Mateo
        Calif. $8,700,000

2/20/2009   Premier Service Bank Riverside   Calif.
        $4,000,000

2/20/2009   Florida Business BancGroup, Inc.   Tampa
        Fla. $9,495,000

2/20/2009   Liberty Shares, Inc.   Hinesville   Ga.
        $17,280,000

2/20/2009   CBB Bancorp   Cartersville   Ga.
        $2,644,000

2/20/2009   Hamilton State Bancshares, Inc.
        Hoschton   Ga. $7,000,000

2/20/2009   Northern States Financial Corporation
Waukegan   Ill. $17,211,000

2/20/2009   First BancTrust Corporation   Paris   Ill.
$7,350,000

2/20/2009   First Merchants Corporation   Muncie
Ind. $116,000,000

2/20/2009   Market Bancorporation, Inc.   New Market
Minn. $2,060,000

2/20/2009   Lafayette Bancorp, Inc.   Oxford
Miss. $1,998,000

2/20/2009   BancPlus Corporation Ridgeland   Miss.
$48,000,000

2/20/2009   Security State Bancshares, Inc.
Charleston   Mont. $12,500,000

2/20/2009   Guaranty Bancorp, Inc.   Woodsville
N.H. $6,920,000

2/20/2009   Royal Bancshares of Pennsylvania, Inc.
Narberth   Pa. $30,407,000

2/20/2009   First Priority Financial Corp.   Malvern
Pa. $4,579,000

2/20/2009   Central Community Corporation
Temple   Texas $22,000,000

2/20/2009   Mid-Wisconsin Financial Services, Inc.
       Medford   Wis. $10,000,000

2/20/2009   Crazy Woman Creek Bancorp, Inc.   Buffalo
       Wyo. $3,100,000

2/27/2009   California Bank of Commerce
       Lafayette   Calif. $4,000,000

2/27/2009   Community Business Bank West
       Sacramento   Calif. $3,976,000

2/27/2009   FNB Bancorp South   San Francisco Calif.
       $12,000,000

2/27/2009   California Bank of Commerce
       Lafayette   Calif. $4,000,000

2/27/2009   Community Business Bank West
       Sacramento   Calif. $3,976,000

2/27/2009   FNB Bancorp South   San Francisco Calif.
       $12,000,000

2/27/2009   Columbine Capital Corp.   Buena Vista
       Colo. $2,260,000

2/27/2009   Columbine Capital Corp.   Buena Vista
       Colo. $2,260,000

2/27/2009   BNC Financial Group, Inc.   New Canaan
       Conn. $4,797,000

2/27/2009   BNC Financial Group, Inc.   New Canaan
      Conn. $4,797,000

2/27/2009   Midtown Bank & Trust Company   Atlanta
      Ga. $5,222,000

2/27/2009   Midtown Bank & Trust Company   Atlanta
      Ga. $5,222,000

2/27/2009   D.L. Evans Bancorp   Burley Idaho
      $19,891,000

2/27/2009   D.L. Evans Bancorp   Burley Idaho
      $19,891,000

2/27/2009   Lakeland Financial Corporation
      Warsaw   Ind. $56,044,000

2/27/2009   Integra Bank Corporation   Evansville
      Ind. $83,586,000

2/27/2009   Lakeland Financial Corporation
      Warsaw   Ind. $56,044,000

2/27/2009   Integra Bank Corporation   Evansville
      Ind. $83,586,000

2/27/2009   National Bancshares, Inc.   Bettendorf
      Iowa $24,664,000

2/27/2009   Green Circle Investments, Inc.   Clive
      Iowa $2,400,000

2/27/2009   National Bancshares, Inc.   Bettendorf Iowa $24,664,000

2/27/2009   Green Circle Investments, Inc.   Clive Iowa $2,400,000

2/27/2009   PSB Financial Corporation   Many La. $9,270,000

2/27/2009   PSB Financial Corporation   Many La. $9,270,000

2/27/2009   Howard Bancorp, Inc. Ellicott City   Md. $5,983,000

2/27/2009   Howard Bancorp, Inc. Ellicott City   Md. $5,983,000

2/27/2009   Private Bancorporation, Inc.   Minneapolis Minn. $4,960,000

2/27/2009   Private Bancorporation, Inc.   Minneapolis Minn. $4,960,000

2/27/2009   First M&F Corporation   Kosciusko Miss. $30,000,000

2/27/2009   First M&F Corporation   Kosciusko Miss. $30,000,000

2/27/2009   Green City Bancshares, Inc.   Green City Mo. $651,000

2/27/2009   Green City Bancshares, Inc.   Green City
      Mo. $651,000

2/27/2009   Catskill Hudson Bancorp, Inc Rock Hill
      N.Y. $3,000,000

2/27/2009   Catskill Hudson Bancorp, Inc Rock Hill
      N.Y. $3,000,000

2/27/2009   First Gothenburg Bancshares, Inc.
      Gothenburg   Neb. $7,570,000

2/27/2009   First Gothenburg Bancshares, Inc.
      Gothenburg   Neb. $7,570,000

2/27/2009   Regent Capital Corporation   Nowata
      Okla. $2,655,000

2/27/2009   Regent Capital Corporation   Nowata
      Okla. $2,655,000

2/27/2009   TriState Capital Holdings, Inc.
      Pittsburgh   Pa. $23,000,000

2/27/2009   The Victory Bank   Limerick   Pa.
      $541,000

2/27/2009   TriState Capital Holdings, Inc.
      Pittsburgh   Pa. $23,000,000

2/27/2009   The Victory Bank   Limerick   Pa.
      $541,000

2/27/2009   Southern First Bancshares, Inc.
Greenville   S.C. $17,299,000

2/27/2009   Southern First Bancshares, Inc.
Greenville   S.C. $17,299,000

2/27/2009   Community First Inc. Columbia   Tenn.
$17,806,000

2/27/2009   Avenue Financial Holdings, Inc.
Nashville   Tenn. $7,400,000

2/27/2009   Community First Inc. Columbia   Tenn.
$17,806,000

2/27/2009   Avenue Financial Holdings, Inc.
Nashville   Tenn. $7,400,000

2/27/2009   First State Bank of Mobeetie Mobeetie
Texas $731,000

2/27/2009   Central Bancorp, Inc. Garland   Texas
$22,500,000

2/27/2009   First State Bank of Mobeetie Mobeetie
Texas $731,000

2/27/2009   Central Bancorp, Inc. Garland   Texas
$22,500,000

2/27/2009   Medallion Bank   Salt Lake City Utah
$11,800,000

2/27/2009	Medallion Bank	Salt Lake City	Utah
$11,800,000

2/27/2009	Ridgestone Financial Services, Inc.
Brookfield	Wis.	$10,900,000

2/27/2009	Ridgestone Financial Services, Inc.
Brookfield	Wis.	$10,900,000

3/6/2009	First Federal Bancshares of Arkansas, Inc.
Harrison	Ark.	$16,500,000

3/6/2009	ICB Financial	Ontario	Calif.
$6,000,000

3/6/2009	First Southwest Bancorporation, Inc.
Alamosa	Colo.	$5,500,000

3/6/2009	Highlands Independent Bancshares, Inc.
Sebring	Fla.	$6,700,000

3/6/2009	Pinnacle Bank Holding Company, Inc.
Orange City	Fla.	$4,389,000

3/6/2009	Marine Bank & Trust Company	Vero
Beach	Fla.	$3,000,000

3/6/2009	Regent Bancorp, Inc.	Davie	Fla.
$9,982,000

3/6/2009	Citizens Bancshares Corporation	Atlanta
Ga.	$7,462,000

3/6/2009   PeoplesSouth Bancshares, Inc.
      Colquitt   Ga. $12,325,000

3/6/2009   First Busey Corporation   Urbana
      Ill. $100,000,000

3/6/2009   Blue River Bancshares, Inc.   Shelbyville
      Ind. $5,000,000

3/6/2009   Community Bancshares of Kansas, Inc.
      Goff   Kan. $500,000

3/6/2009   Blue Ridge Bancshares, Inc.   Independence
      Mo. $12,000,000

3/6/2009   AmeriBank Holding Company
      Collinsville   Okla. $2,492,000

3/6/2009   HCSB Financial Corporation   Loris   S.C.
      $12,895,000

3/6/2009   First Reliance Bancshares, Inc.
      Florence   S.C. $15,349,000

3/6/2009   Merchants and Planters Bancshares, Inc.
      Toone   Tenn. $1,881,000

3/6/2009   Germantown Capital Corporation, Inc.
      Germantown   Tenn. $4,967,000

3/6/2009   First Texas BHC, Inc.   Fort Worth   Texas
      $13,533,000

3/6/2009   Farmers & Merchants Bancshares, Inc.
Houston   Texas $11,000,000

3/6/2009   BOH Holdings, Inc.   Houston   Texas
$10,000,000

3/6/2009   Park Bancorporation, Inc.   Madison
Wis. $23,200,000

3/13/2009   BancIndependent, Inc.   Sheffield
Ala. $21,100,000

3/13/2009   First Northern Community Bancorp   Dixon
Calif. $17,390,000

3/13/2009   Salisbury Bancorp, Inc.   Lakeville
Conn. $8,816,000

3/13/2009   1st United Bancorp, Inc.   Boca Raton
Fla. $10,000,000

3/13/2009   First Intercontinental Bank   Doraville
Ga. $6,398,000

3/13/2009   Discover Financial Services   Riverwoods
Ill. $1,224,558,000

3/13/2009   Butler Point, Inc.   Catlin   Ill.
$607,000

3/13/2009   Haviland Bancshares, Inc.   Haviland
Kan. $425,000

3/13/2009   Madison Financial Corporation
        Richmond   Ky. $3,370,000

3/13/2009   St. Johns Bancshares, Inc.   St. Louis
        Mo. $3,000,000

3/13/2009   First American International Corp.
        Brooklyn   N.Y. $17,000,000

3/13/2009   IBW Financial Corporation   Washington
DC   n/a $6,000,000

3/13/2009   Bank of George   Las Vegas   Nev.
        $2,672,000

3/13/2009   First Place Financial Corp.   Warren
        Ohio $72,927,000

3/13/2009   Provident Community Bancshares, Inc.
        Rock Hill   S.C. $9,266,000

3/13/2009   Moneytree Corporation   Lenoir City
        Tenn. $9,516,000

3/13/2009   Sovereign Bancshares, Inc.   Dallas Texas
        $18,215,000

3/13/2009   First National Corporation   Strasburg
        Va. $13,900,000

3/13/2009   Blackhawk Bancorp, Inc.   Beloit Wis.
        $10,000,000

3/20/2009   Heritage Oaks Bancorp   Paso Robles
Calif. $21,000,000

3/20/2009   Premier Bank Holding Company
Tallahassee   Fla. $9,500,000

3/20/2009   Farmers & Merchants Financial Corporation
Argonia   Kan. $442,000

3/20/2009   Farmers State Bankshares, Inc.   Holton
Kan. $700,000

3/20/2009   First NBC Bank Holding Company   New
Orleans   La. $17,836,000

3/20/2009   Citizens Bank & Trust Company
Covington   La. $2,400,000

3/20/2009   Kirksville Bancorp, Inc.   Kirksville
Mo. $470,000

3/20/2009   First Colebrook Bancorp, Inc. Colebrook
N.H. $4,500,000

3/20/2009   Community First Bancshares Inc.   Union
City   Tenn. $20,000,000

3/20/2009   Peoples Bancshares of TN, Inc.
Madisonville   Tenn. $3,900,000

3/27/2009   SBT Bancorp, Inc.   Simsbury   Conn.
$4,000,000

3/27/2009   CSRA Bank Corp.   Wrens Ga.
$2,400,000

3/27/2009   Trinity Capital Corporation   Los Alamos
N.M. $35,539,000

3/27/2009   Clover Community Bankshares, Inc. Clover
S.C. $3,000,000

3/27/2009   Pathway Bancorp   Cairo   Neb.
$3,727,000

3/27/2009   Colonial American Bank West
Conshohocken   Pa. $574,000

3/27/2009   MS Financial, Inc.   Kingwood   Texas
$7,723,000

3/27/2009   Triad Bancorp, Inc.   Frontenac   Mo.
$3,700,000

3/27/2009   Alpine Banks of Colorado   Glenwood
Springs   Colo. $70,000,000

3/27/2009   Naples Bancorp, Inc. Naples Fla.
$4,000,000

3/27/2009   CBS Banc-Corp.   Russellville   Ala.
$24,300,000

3/27/2009   IBT Bancorp, Inc.   Irving Texas
$2,295,000

3/27/2009   Spirit BankCorp, Inc.   Bristow   Okla.
    $30,000,000

3/27/2009   Maryland Financial Bank   Towson
        Md. $1,700,000

4/3/2009   First Capital Bancorp, Inc.   Glen Ellen
        Va. $10,958,000

4/3/2009   Tri-State Bank of Memphis   Memphis
        Tenn. $2,795,000

4/3/2009   Fortune Financial Corporation   Arnold
        Mo. $3,100,000

4/3/2009   BancStar, Inc. Festus Mo. $8,600,000

4/3/2009   Titonka Bancshares, Inc   Titonka
        Iowa $2,117,000

4/3/2009   Millennium Bancorp, Inc.   Edwards
        Colo. $7,260,000

4/3/2009   TriSummit Bank   Kingsport   Tenn.
    $2,765,000

4/3/2009   Prairie Star Bancshares, Inc. Olathe Kan.
    $2,800,000

4/3/2009   Community First Bancshares, Inc.
        Harrison   Ark. $12,725,000

4/3/2009   BCB Holding Company, Inc.   Theodore
        Ala. $1,706,000

4/10/2009   City National Bancshares Corporation
        Newark   N.J. $9,439,000

4/10/2009   First Business Bank, N.A.   San Diego
        Calif. $2,211,000

4/10/2009   SV Financial, Inc.   Sterling   Ill.
        $4,000,000

4/10/2009   Capital Commerce Bancorp, Inc.
        Milwaukee   Wis. $5,100,000

4/10/2009   Metropolitan Capital Bancorp, Inc.
        Chicago   Ill. $2,040,000

4/17/2009   Bank of the Carolinas Corporation
        Mocksville   N.C. $13,179,000

4/17/2009   Penn Liberty Financial Corp.   Wayne
        Pa. $9,960,000

4/17/2009   Tifton Banking Company   Tifton Ga.
        $3,800,000

4/17/2009   Patterson Bancshares, Inc   Patterson
        La. $3,690,000

4/17/2009   BNB Financial Services Corporation   New
York   N.Y. $7,500,000

4/17/2009   Omega Capital Corp. Lakewood   Colo.
        $2,816,000

4/24/2009   Mackinac Financial Corporation / mBank
Manistique   Mich. $11,000,000

4/24/2009   Birmingham Bloomfield Bancshares, Inc
Birmingham   Mich. $1,635,000

4/24/2009   Vision Bank - Texas   Richardson   Texas
$1,500,000

4/24/2009   Oregon Bancorp, Inc.   Salem   Ore.
$3,216,000

4/24/2009   Peoples Bancorporation, Inc.   Easley   S.C.
$12,660,000

4/24/2009   Indiana Bank Corp.   Dana   Ind.
$1,312,000

4/24/2009   Business Bancshares, Inc.   Clayton
Mo. $15,000,000

4/24/2009   Standard Bancshares, Inc.   Hickory Hills
Ill. $60,000,000

4/24/2009   York Traditions Bank   York   Pa.
$4,871,000

4/24/2009   Grand Capital Corporation   Tulsa   Okla.
$4,000,000

4/24/2009   Allied First Bancorp, Inc.   Oswego
Ill. $3,652,000

4/24/2009   Frontier Bancshares, Inc.   Austin Texas
$3,000,000

5/1/2009   Village Bank and Trust Financial Corp.
Midlothian   Va. $14,738,000

5/1/2009   CenterBank   Milford   Ohio
$2,250,000

5/1/2009   Georgia Primary Bank   Atlanta
Ga. $4,500,000

5/1/2009   Union Bank & Trust Company   Oxford
N.C. $3,194,000

5/1/2009   HPK Financial Corporation   Chicago
Ill. $4,000,000

5/1/2009   OSB Financial Services, Inc.   Orange
Texas $6,100,000

5/1/2009   Security State Bank Holding-Company
Jamestown   N.D. $10,750,000

5/8/2009   Highlands State Bank Vernon   N.J.
$3,091,000

5/8/2009   One Georgia Bank   Atlanta   Ga.
$5,500,000

5/8/2009   Gateway Bancshares, Inc.   Ringgold
Ga. $6,000,000

5/8/2009   Freeport Bancshares, Inc.   Freeport
     Ill. $3,000,000

5/8/2009   Investors Financial Corporation of Pettis
County, Inc.   Sedalia   Mo. $4,000,000

5/8/2009   Sword Financial Corporation   Horicon
     Wis. $13,644,000

5/8/2009   Premier Bancorp, Inc. Wilmette   Ill.
     $6,784,000

5/15/2009   Mercantile Bank Corporation   Grand
Rapids Mich. $21,000,000

5/15/2009   Northern State Bank   Closter   N.J.
     $1,341,000

5/15/2009   Western Reserve Bancorp, Inc
     Medina   Ohio $4,700,000

5/15/2009   Community Financial Shares, Inc.   Glen
Ellyn   Ill. $6,970,000

5/15/2009   Worthington Financial Holdings, Inc.
     Huntsville   Ala. $2,720,000

5/15/2009   First Community Bancshares, Inc
     Overland Park Kan. $14,800,000

5/15/2009   Southern Heritage Bancshares, Inc.
     Cleveland   Tenn. $4,862,000

5/15/2009   Foresight Financial Group, Inc.
Rockford   Ill. $15,000,000

5/15/2009   IBC Bancorp, Inc.   Chicago   Ill.
$4,205,000

5/15/2009   Boscobel Bancorp, Inc   Boscobel
Wis. $5,586,000

5/15/2009   Brogan Bankshares, Inc.   Kaukauna
Wis. $2,400,000

5/15/2009   Riverside Bancshares, Inc.   Little Rock
Ark. $1,100,000

5/15/2009   Deerfield Financial Corporation
Deerfield   Wis. $2,639,000

5/15/2009   Market Street Bancshares, Inc.   Mt.
Vernon   Ill. $20,300,000

5/22/2009   The Landrum Company   Columbia
Mo.. $15,000,000

5/22/2009   First Advantage Bancshares Inc.   Coon
Rapids Minn. $1,177,000

5/22/2009   Fort Lee Federal Savings Bank   Fort
Lee   N.J. $1,300,000

5/22/2009   Blackridge Financial, Inc.   Fargo   N.D.
$5,000,000

5/22/2009   Illinois State Bancorp, Inc.   Chicago
     Ill. $6,272,000

5/22/2009   Universal Bancorp   Bloomfield   Ind.
     $9,900,000

5/22/2009   Franklin Bancorp, Inc.   Washington
     Mo. $5,097,000

5/22/2009   Commonwealth Bancshares, Inc.
     Louisville   Ky. $20,400,000

5/22/2009   Premier Financial Corp   Dubuque
     Iowa $6,349,000

5/22/2009   F & C Bancorp, Inc.   Holden   Mo.
     $2,993,000

5/22/2009   Diamond Bancorp, Inc.   Washington
     Mo. $20,445,000

5/22/2009   United Bank Corporation   Barnesville
     Ga. $14,400,000

5/29/2009   Community Bank Shares of Indiana, Inc.
     New Albany   Ind. $19,468,000

5/29/2009   American Premier Bancorp   Arcadia
     Calif. $1,800,000

5/29/2009   CB Holding Corp.   Aledo   Ill.
     $4,114,000

5/29/2009   Citizens Bancshares Co.   Chillicothe
        Mo. $24,990,000

5/29/2009   Grand Mountain Bancshares, Inc.   Granby
        Colo. $3,076,000

5/29/2009   Two Rivers Financial Group   Burlington
        Iowa $12,000,000

5/29/2009   Fidelity Bancorp, Inc   Baton Rouge   La.
        $3,942,000

5/29/2009   Chambers Bancshares, Inc.   Danville
        Ark. $19,817,000

6/5/2009   Covenant Financial Corporation
        Clarksdale   Miss. $5,000,000

6/5/2009   First Trust Corporation   New Orleans
        La. $17,969,000

6/5/2009   OneFinancial Corporation   Little Rock
        Ark. $17,300,000

6/12/2009   Berkshire Bancorp, Inc.   Wyomissing
        Pa. $2,892,000

6/12/2009   First Vernon Bancshares, Inc. Vernon
        Ala. $6,000,000

6/12/2009   SouthFirst Bancshares, Inc.   Sylacauga
        Ala. $2,760,000

6/12/2009   Virginia Company Bank   Newport News   Va. $4,700,000

6/12/2009   Enterprise Financial Services Group, Inc.
        Allison Park   Pa. $4,000,000

6/12/2009   First Financial Bancshares, Inc.
        Lawrence   Kan. $3,756,000

6/12/2009   River Valley Bancorporation, Inc.
        Wausau   Wis. $15,000,000

6/12/2009   Berkshire Bancorp, Inc.   Wyomissing
        Pa. $2,892,000

6/12/2009   First Vernon Bancshares, Inc. Vernon
        Ala. $6,000,000

6/12/2009   SouthFirst Bancshares, Inc.   Sylacauga
        Ala. $2,760,000

6/12/2009   Virginia Company Bank   Newport News   Va. $4,700,000

6/12/2009   Enterprise Financial Services Group, Inc.
        Allison Park   Pa. $4,000,000

6/12/2009   First Financial Bancshares, Inc.
        Lawrence   Kan. $3,756,000

6/12/2009   River Valley Bancorporation, Inc.
        Wausau   Wis. $15,000,000

6/19/2009   Merchants and Manufacturers Bank
Corporation   Joliet   Ill. $3,510,000

6/19/2009   RCB Financial Corporation   Rome   Ga.
    $8,900,000

6/19/2009   Manhattan Bancshares, Inc.   Manhattan
    Ill. $2,639,000

6/19/2009   Biscayne Bancshares, Inc.   Coconut
Grove   Fla. $6,400,000

6/19/2009   Duke Financial Group, Inc.   Minneapolis
    Minn. $12,000,000

6/19/2009   Farmers Enterprises, Inc.   Great Bend
    Kan. $12,000,000

6/19/2009   Century Financial Services Corporation
    Santa Fe   N.M. $10,000,000

6/19/2009   NEMO Bancshares Inc.   Madison
    Mo. $2,330,000

6/19/2009   University Financial Corp, Inc.   St.
Paul   Minn. $11,926,000

6/19/2009   Suburban Illinois Bancorp, Inc.
    Elmhurst   Ill. $15,000,000

6/26/2009   Hartford Financial Services Group, Inc.
    Hartford   Conn. $3,400,000,000

6/26/2009   Fidelity Resources Company   Plano   Texas $3,000,000

6/26/2009   Waukesha Bankshares, Inc.   Waukesha   Wis. $5,625,000

6/26/2009   FC Holdings, Inc.   Houston   Texas $21,042,000

6/26/2009   Security Capital Corporation   Batesville   Miss. $17,388,000

6/26/2009   First Alliance Bancshares, Inc.   Cordova   Tenn. $3,422,000

6/26/2009   Gulfstream Bancshares, Inc.   Stuart   Fla. $7,500,000

6/26/2009   Gold Canyon Bank   Gold   Canyon   Ariz. $1,607,000

6/26/2009   M&F Bancorp, Inc.   Durham   N.C. $11,735,000

6/26/2009   Metropolitan Bank Group, Inc.   Chicago   Ill. $71,526,000

6/26/2009   NC Bancorp, Inc.   Chicago   Ill. $6,880,000

6/26/2009   Alliance Bancshares, Inc.   Dalton   Ga. $2,986,000

6/26/2009   Stearns Financial Services, Inc.   St. Cloud   Minn. $24,900,000

6/26/2009   Signature Bancshares, Inc.   Dallas   Texas $1,700,000

6/26/2009   Fremont Bancorporation   Fremont   Calif. $35,000,000

6/26/2009   Alliance Financial Services Inc.   St. Paul   Minn. $12,000,000

7/10/2009   Lincoln National Corporation   Radnor   Pa. $950,000,000

7/10/2009   Bancorp Financial, Inc.   Oak Brook   Ill. $13,669,000

7/17/2009   Brotherhood Bancshares, Inc.   Kansas City   Kan. $11,000,000

7/17/2009   SouthCrest Financial Group, Inc.   Fayetteville   Ga. $12,900,000

7/17/2009   Harbor Bankshares Corporation   Baltimore   Md. $6,800,000

7/17/2009   First South Bancorp, Inc.   Lexington   Tenn. $50,000,000

7/17/2009   Great River Holding Company   Baxter   Minn. $8,400,000

7/17/2009   Plato Holdings Inc.   St. Paul   Minn.
$2,500,000

7/24/2009   Yadkin Valley Financial Corp. Elkin   N.C.
$13,312,000

7/24/2009   Community Bancshares, Inc. Kingman
Ariz. $3,872,000

7/24/2009   Florida Bank Group, Inc.   Tampa Fla.
$20,471,000

7/24/2009   First American Bank Corp.   Elk Grove
Village Ill. $50,000,000

7/31/2009   Chicago Shore Corp.   Chicago   Ill.
$7,000,000

7/31/2009   Financial Services of Winger, Inc.   Winger
Minn. $3,742,000

8/7/2009   The ANB Corporation Terrell Texas
$20,000,000

8/7/2009   U.S. Century Bank   Miami Fla.
$50,236,000

8/14/2009   Bank Financial Services, Inc.   Eden Prarie
Minn. $1,004,000

8/21/2009   KS Bancorp Inc.   Smithfield   N.C.
$4,000,000

8/21/2009   AmFirst Financial Services Inc.
      McCook   Neb. $5,000,000

8/28/2009   First Independence Corp.   Detroit
      Mich. $3,223,000

8/28/2009   First Guaranty Bancshares Inc.
      Hammond   La. $20,699,000

8/28/2009   CoastalSouth Bancshares Inc.   Hilton
Head Island   S.C. $16,015,000

8/28/2009   TCB Corporation   Greenwood   S.C.
      $9,720,000

9/4/2009   The State Bank of Bartley   Bartley
      Neb. $1,697,000

9/11/2009   Pathfinder Bancorp, Inc.   Oswego
      N.Y. $6,771,000

9/11/2009   Community Bancshares of Mississippi, Inc.
      Brandon   Miss. $52,000,000

9/11/2009   Heartland Bancshares, Inc.   Franklin
      Ind. $7,000,000

9/11/2009   PFSB Bancorporation, Inc.   Pigeon Falls
      Wis. $1,500,000

9/11/2009   First Eagle Bancshares, Inc.   Hanover Park
      Ill. $7,500,000

9/18/2009   IA Bancorp, Inc.   Iselin   N.J.
$5,976,000

9/18/2009   HomeTown Bankshares Corporation
Roanoke   Va. $10,000,000

9/25/2009   Heritage Bankshares Inc.   Norfolk
Va. $10,103,000

9/25/2009   Mountain Valley Bancshares   Cleveland
Ga. $3,300,000

9/25/2009   Grand Financial Corp. Hattiesburg   Miss.
$2,443,320

9/25/2009   Guaranty Capital Corp.   Belzoni
Miss. $14,000,000

9/25/2009   GulfSouth Private Bank   Destin Fla.
$7,500,000

9/25/2009   Steele Street Bank Corp.   Denver
Colo. $11,019,000

10/2/2009   Premier Financial Bancorp   Huntington
W.Va. $22,252,000

10/2/2009   Providence Bank   Rocky Mount   N.C.
$4,000,000

10/23/2009   Regents Bancshares   Vancouver   Wash.
$12,700,000

10/23/2009   Cardinal Bancorp II   Washington   Mo.
$6,251,000

10/30/2009   Randolph Bank & Trust Co.   Asheboro
N.C.. $6,229,000

10/30/2009   WashingtonFirst Bankshares Reston
Va. $6,842,000

11/6/2009   F & M Bancshares   Trezevant   Tenn.
$3,535,000

11/20/2009   Presidio Bank San Francisco Calif.
$10,800,000

11/20/2009   McLeod Bancshares   Shorewood   Minn.
$6,000,000

11/20/2009   Metropolitan Capital Bancorp
Chicago   Ill. $2,348,000

12/4/2009   Broadway Financial Corp.   Los Angeles
Calif. $6,000,000

12/4/2009   Delmar Bancorp   Delmar   Md.
$9,000,000

12/4/2009   Liberty Bancshares   Fort Worth   Texas
$6,500,000

Total purchase amount: $204,808,576,320

Total repaid: -$96,249,045,000

Capital Purchase Program total investment:
$108,487,042,320

Source:
http://money.cnn.com/news/specials/storysupplement/b
ankbailout/